"AGENTS PRACTICE A SECRET CRAFT,
THEY TRY TO KEEP IT THAT WAY. . . ."

The Dictionary of Espionage is an attempt to interpret the language the espionage community uses in talking to and about itself. Much of the information in the following pages was gleaned from agents, both active and retired, who served the world's major spy organizations. There are also some sidetrips into intelligence trivia, the oddball facts with which operatives entertain themselves while at rest. Tradecraft dictates that I not give formal acknowledgments to the persons who contributed to this book. . . ."

—Henry S. A. Becket
From the Introduction

"USEFUL TO ANY SERIOUS STUDENT OF ESPIONAGE."

—*Wilson Library Bulletin*

"ANYONE INTERESTED IN LANGUAGE WILL FIND *THE DICTIONARY OF ESPIONAGE* INFORMATIVE."

—*Publishers Weekly*

THE DICTIONARY OF ESPIONAGE

Spookspeak into English

Henry S. A. Becket

A DELL BOOK

Published by
Dell Publishing Co., Inc.
1 Dag Hammarskjold Plaza
New York, New York 10017

Dell ® TM 681510, Dell Publishing Co., Inc.

ISBN: 0-440-11955-3

Reprinted by arrangement with Stein and Day, Inc.

Printed in the United States of America

August 1987

7 6 5 4 3 2 1

For the Bearess of the Flagship,
Who speaks spook and other languages
As well; with love from your
Perpetual Shipmate

A Prelude

How hath the spy dwelt so long amongst us? What is his utility to the state and the citizenry? How is he considered—and known—by the people he serves, often at the risk to his life? He is at once rogue and useful fellow. We survive by his information, yet we taunt and abuse him, and we have scant knowledge of his theories and his tactics; yea, we do not even speak his tongue. So let us examine our society's surrogate, commencing with his origins and purposes, and then proceeding to the manner by which he addresses his very own.

Introduction

Spies speak their own language. This is no accident. Agents practice a secret craft, and they wish and they try to keep it that way. The purpose of a priestly private language is severalfold. It fends off outsiders, or at least leaves them uncertain as to what is being said around them. Learning the language is one of the first lessons addressed by an apprentice agent. Writing of his tradecraft* training at the CIA's facility at Camp Peary, Virginia, during the early 1950s, longtime Agency officer Joseph Burkholder Smith explained, "At the same time this vocabulary was taught, we were warned never to use it except among ourselves and with agents under secure circumstances, because its use would identify us as spies. Obviously, learning the language of espionage was partly a familiarization with the tools of the trade and *partly an initiation rite.*" (Emphasis added.) Another CIA veteran, the pseudonymous Christopher Felix, said much the same in his memoir: "The purpose of secret operations [is] obscured by the existence of a professional lingo which—like all technical language—is used by professionals for greater precision and misused popularly to the confusion of the layman."

These men, however, were trained decades ago, in an era when the world's intelligence agencies still operated in relative secrecy. Such is no longer the case. Intelligence is spawning its own professional and popular literature (indeed, the two agents cited above have published accounts of their espionage experiences). The public reads the language of spookdom in hundreds of thriller novels annually. The Church Committee of the U.S. Senate, which poked through CIA's closets for two years during the 1970s, was so intrigued with the peculiar language used in the American intelligence community that it felt compelled to

---

* Itself a precise term; see definition herein.

include a fourteen-page glossary in its final report. Spookspeak is now part of the daily babble that comes to our ears.

But does the lay citizen understand what he is hearing or reading? I think not. Nor, for that matter, does veteran CIA officer David Atlee Phillips, who in retirement formed the Association of Former Intelligence Officers in an attempt to promote better public understanding of intelligence issues and functions. During the ongoing debate on how a democratic and "open" society should conduct secret operations, Phillips told the Church Committee, "subject matters and issues were being obscured—if not lost—in an esoteric jargon borrowed by Congress and the media from the intelligence subcultures. As with most trade talk, intelligence terminology such as clandestine operations, covert action and black box is highly technical and has developed nuances not easily inferred from the words themselves." Spookspeak is a lively and derivative language, and rival services borrow and adapt one another's terminology. They have also reached into antiquity for the precise word for a practice they wish to describe.

A good example: In 1974 the British novelist John le Carré sent his indefatigable counterintelligence officer George Smiley in quest of a Soviet agent who had penetrated British intelligence. Le Carré called this agent a "mole." The word struck popular fancy, even within the intelligence community, and officers soon used it as their very own (although even such an esteemed CIA veteran as William Hood noted he had never heard it pre-le Carré). Then Walter Pforzheimer, retired CIA legislative counsel and the foremost intelligence bibliophile in the world, began poking into history, and he discovered the crafty le Carré actually was using a term 350 years old. Sir Francis Bacon had written, in a 1622 biography of King Henry VII, that "Hee was careful and liberall to obtaine good Intelligence from all parts abroad. . . . He had such Moles perpetually working and casting to undermine him." Thus does a spookspeak term lie dormant for centuries, awaiting reentry into the language of espionage.

The Dictionary of Espionage is an attempt to interpret the language the espionage community uses in talking to and about itself. Much of the information in the following pages was gleaned from agents, both active and retired, who served the world's major spy organizations. There are also some sidetrips into intelligence trivia, the oddball facts with which operatives entertain themselves while at rest. Tradecraft dictates that I not give formal acknowledgments to the persons who contributed to this book. The major printed sources are found in the bibliography.

—Henry S. A. Becket
April 30, 1985

a

ACCESS PERMIT

The document that gives Soviet intelligence agents permission to deal with classified material in the course of their work. The permit spells out specific security procedures. According to A. I. Romanov, a former Soviet intelligence officer who defected, the gist of the permit is as follows: "If I am handed a secret document, I must sign for it in a special book, giving date and time of day, in the presence of the person responsible for the safekeeping of such documents. I must not allow this document to be out of my sight even for a moment, must not put it in my pocket, on a table, or in my briefcase, must not make a copy of it or write down any extracts from it, nor discuss its contents with anyone at all. After reading it, or, as they used to say in the NKVD, absorbing it, I had to hand it back personally to the man who had issued it."

The exchange is formally noted in a control ledger, with stamps and documents. The agreement notes that the penalty for violations could be death. U.S. and Soviet intelligence schools follow a parallel course in impressing fledgling agents with the seriousness of security: a marginal student in each class is detected in a security violation and rather noisily dismissed from the school. This happened at midcourse of my training at the Army Intelligence School in Baltimore in 1956; the poor wretch who left a classified manual atop a filing cabinet was sent to Fort Dix for infantry training—a fate whose discomforts were not lost on the rest of us.

ACCOMMODATION ADDRESS

A location where an agent can receive mail, even though he does not reside there or have any visible connection with anyone who does. Small European shops traditionally have received mail for transients, for a minimal fee. The FBI utilizes established corporations, where mail directed to a particular individual or department is shunted to a designated pickup point. Because of the mail pilferage endemic to the U.S. postal system, Soviet agents no longer rely upon post office boxes as accommodation addresses, according to a counterintelligence expert on KGB affairs. The KGB now utilizes the plethora of "private post offices" that offer rentals for $10 or so monthly, with no requirement of identification.

The KGB used one such service for more than a year in the 1960s, not knowing that the supposed owner actually worked for a U.S. intelligence agency. Much of the material transmitted through this particular drop was said to be "low-grade," but the agency did acquire several "useful leads." The mail service eventually closed because of circumstances beyond the control of the agency.

ACTIVE MEASURES (aktivnyye meropriyatiya)

A Soviet term used to refer to operations intended to influence or otherwise affect other nations' policies. According to a CIA internal memorandum published in 1982, active measures, both covert and overt, consist of a broad range of activities, including "manipulation or control of the media; written or oral disinformation; use of foreign Communist parties or organizations; manipulation of mass organizations; clandestine radio broadcasting; economic activities, military operations, and other political influence operations. . . . These operations have a common aim: to insinuate Soviet policy views into foreign governmental, journalistic, business, labor, academic, and artistic opinion in a nonattributable fashion." *(See also* DISINFORMATION.)

AGENT

In current usage, a person who engages in spying or the support of those who do, or who seeks to detect them. Oddly, the word is one that professional intelligence operatives seldom apply to themselves. A CIA man working abroad as a spy would call himself an "officer," although the persons who worked for him (non-CIA men or women) would be called agents. In the American context, the differentiation began during World War II, when the Office of Strategic Services drew a careful distinction between its very own people and others. According to OSS manuals, an *operative* was "an individual employed by and responsible to the OSS and assigned under special programs to field activity." An *agent*, by contrast, was "an individual recruited in the field who is employed or directed by an OSS operative or by a field or substation."

FBI draws no such distinction; its officers are not only agents, they are *special* agents, and they so introduce and identify themselves. The late director J. Edgar Hoover insisted upon the distinguishing adjective as a means of setting his men apart from run-of-the-mill cops (Hoover didn't hire female agents until near the end of his reign.) The Dallas trial lawyer William F. Alexander delighted in opening his cross-examination of FBI witnesses this way: "Well, special agent Jones, what's so *special* about you?"

AGENT 86

The code name for Maximilian Smart in the TV spy spoof, "Get Smart." The inside joke is that 86 is restaurant code for having run out of something—"Mabel, eighty-six on the tapioca."

AGENT ENVIRONMENT
See OPERATIONAL CLIMATE.

AGENT-IN-PLACE

Perhaps the rarest and most valuable of intelligence persons —the agent who is recruited by a foreign power, and who agrees to continue in his position so that the information he passes is current and valuable. Fatalism is presumed by both sides, for agents-in-place face horrible fates if detected. By reliable account a KGB traitor was thrust into a roaring furnace, feet first, while more than a hundred of his colleagues watched. The lesson was obvious.

AGENT OF INFLUENCE

A person not directly under control of an intelligence agency, but willing to work on its behalf. As former CIA official David Atlee Phillips told the Church Committee, "He might be a radio commentator or a local Bernard Baruch whose park bench opin-

ions carry political weight. The agent of influence might be the
foreign minister's mistress. Most covert activities utilizing the
agent of influence are useful to American ambassadors in
achieving low-key but important objectives of U.S. foreign policy. These activities are known in intelligence jargon as 'moth-
erhood,' and revelations concerning them would not shock or
disturb the Amercian public."

Because of widespread government corruption, agents of influence are easily acquirable in Latin America. The Spanish colonial tradition was that the king (of Spain) "owned" the government, hence he or his subordinate is entitled to payment for
any routine service. Officials who routinely accept the *mordida*
(little bite, or payoff) for doing their jobs see no harm in taking
money from an intelligence officer: if the agent wants the information, and has sufficient pesos, the information is his. In one
Latin country in the 1960s, an agent so cultivated such a
"friend" that every document that entered or left his office was
routinely copied and given to the CIA station. The cost was the
equivalent of two bottles of Scotch monthly.

Another former CIA official, E. Howard Hunt, defined the
agent of influence as "either a government official so highly
placed that he can exercise influence on government policy or
an opinion molder so influential as to be capable of altering the
attitudes of an entire country." In the case of a Soviet agent of
influence, "though his politics may be of the left, he is not—
and cannot be known as—a Communist."

The KGB uses the same term as CIA, a literal translation from
the Russian *agent vlyiyania*. A large portion of covert KGB intelligence work in the United States and elsewhere is devoted to
handling such agents, who are not spies in the classic sense, and
often do not even realize they are being used by a foreign
power. But KGB singles them out for cultivation because of
their ability to exert influence in their societies—professors,
government officials, politicians, journalists, labor leaders, fi-
nanciers, and industrialists. The approaches are low-key. The
KGB officer, for instance, suggests to an American businessman
that United States trade policy means loss of profitable USSR
markets to the Europeans; could he not say something to his
friends in Washington about a change? Or a "visiting Soviet
academician" has a background lunch with Washington journalists, and argues that a shift in American bargaining positions

on arms talks would bring commensurate concessions from the USSR. His statement is publicized as a "softening" of Soviet position that should be matched by the United States. (Both these "examples" actually happened.)

"The run-of-the-mill influence agents recruited by the KGB in the capitalist world must by now run into the hundreds," the CIA Soviet specialist Harry Rositzke wrote in 1981. "It is difficult to determine in many cases the variety of motivations that induce them to 'cooperate' with their Soviet friends. Political and commercial opportunism plays a part. Some may have genuine political sympathies with the Soviet side of the Cold War confrontation. . . . Some no doubt have been blackmailed."

AGENT PROVOCATEUR

A person who insinuates himself into an organization with the aim of inciting it to acts that would make its members subject to punishment. In 1950s CIA usage, such an agent was a "tree-shaker," a person who would join an organization with the intent of seeing if its timetable could be accelerated, and what its actual plans were. An agent provocateur is an archvillain of labor and revolutionary history, and the genre does have an odious tradition.

AGIT-PROP

Agitation and propaganda, generally used in reference to Communist and Front Group activities. Agit-prop involves the dramatic protrayal of an issue—mass marches, exhortatory speeches, and events crafted to attract media attention. For instance, in 1967 the underground newspaper *East Village Other* intended to drop two hundred pounds of flowers on the Pentagon from an airplane to signify support of an anti-war march. An agent in the New York FBI field office answered an advertisement for a pilot, and kept up the pretense to the point where the publisher arrived at the airport with the flowers. No pilot, no flight, no dropped flowers. As the field office boasted in a memo to FBI headquarters in Washington, the agent thus was able to prevent "agit-prop activity as it relates to dropping flowers over Washington." Another agit-prop stunt went awry in Washington in July 1982. Opponents of the regime in El Salvador had fatigue-clad soldiers "enact" the seizure of innocent peasant women by jumping from a truck downtown and grabbing persons (accomplices) from a crowd. The organizers did not bother to inform the Washington police of the stunt: when the soldiers grabbed the women, they in turn were quickly grabbed, handcuffed, and spreadeagled by officers.

ALL-SKATE
See FLOATING CONTACT.

AMTORG

A Soviet trading corporation set up in New York in the 1930s. In one sense, Amtorg was a genuine commercial enterprise that did hundreds of millions of dollars in business with leading American corporations. But this brisk activity also gave invaluable cover to hordes of Soviet intelligence agents. Amtorg provided these agents with jobs as "legal cover," and assigned them to visit various cities and industrial plants, as would any normal commercial travelers. They spied, bought documents, recruited agents—in sum, worked with a free hand. Of the seven hundred to eight hundred Amtorg employees in the mid-1930s, perhaps half were also members of the American Communist Party. There were occasional spy scandals, angry resignations by loyal and unwitting Americans who had gone to work for Amtorg. (One such person, Basil W. Douglas, one-time Amtorg vice-president, said angrily after his resignation: "I have seen information regarding the army and naval defenses of the United States that has been gathered by Amtorg's agents and transmitted to Russia.") But given the vast scope of Amtorg's economic activities, American officials tended to excuse such transgressions as "minor matters."

ANGELS

Popular derogatory name for agents of the Sandinista secret police of Nicaragua, circa 1984. The angels control *turbas divinas,* "divine mobs," who circle the homes of opponents of the Sandinista regime at night, beating sticks against cans and chanting threatening slogans. The *turbas* learned the harassing tactic from the Somoza secret police.

APOSTLES

A lively Cambridge club of the late 1920s and early 1930s that attracted Communists and homosexuals. Two of its most prominent members were the Soviet spies Guy Burgess and Donald Maclean.

ARCOS

The Soviet trade mission in London during the 1920s, closed after its exposure as a spy center. Arcos played much the same role in Britain as its sister organization, Amtorg, did in the United States. *(See also* AMTORG.)

ARMORER

KGB deep-cover agent whose chief purpose is to pass smuggled weapons to terrorists and other groups who work for the Soviets, either wittingly or unwittingly.

ATTORNEY GENERAL'S LIST

A list of subversive organizations first compiled by the Justice Department in the 1930s as a guide to evaluate applicants for Federal employment. Both the criteria for inclusion and the names of the groups have changed frequently over the years. In 1965, the U.S. Supreme Court ruled that requiring individuals to register as members of the cited groups was unconstitutional, as a violation of the privilege against self-incrimination. Thus federal agencies were forced to individually evaluate information regarding membership in allegedly subversive organizations based on raw data furnished by the FBI. The Nixon administration rewrote guidelines for the attorney general's list (in 1971) to redefine "subversive." Executive Order 11605 reads in part:

> . . . totalitarian, fascist, communist, or subversive, or which has adopted a policy of unlawfully advocating the commission of acts of force or violence to deny others their rights under the Constitution or laws of the United States or any state, or which seeks to overthrow the government of the United States or any state or subdivision thereof by unlawful means.

ATTORNEY GENERAL'S PORTFOLIO

The Justice Department's secret plans (since abandoned) for emergency detention of citizens and aliens in time of national emergency. The key element was the FBI's so-called "Security Index" of names of persons to be detained. The Portfolio also contained specific federal facilities at which the persons were to be held and draft "national emergency" orders to be signed by the President giving legal authority to the arrests. According to FBI internal memoranda disclosed by the Church Committee, the FBI would have discretion over who should be listed for detention.

AUNT MINNIES

Photographs taken by professional photographers, journalists, amateurs, or tourists that show a place of interest to an intelligence topographer. These are named after the proverbial "maiden aunt" whose half-obscured head does not block the view of a winding road or a beach or the quaint little whitewashed church that an artillery targeting officer might find of value. OSS had a special section during World War II that scoured antique and secondhand shops for Aunt Minnie postcards.

AUSSTEIGEN

In German, "getting out"; in espionage usage, getting out from under the cover of a Soviet passport and acquiring new travel documentation falsified by the astute "cobblers" in a Berlin "workshop" run by Soviet intelligence. (See also COBBLER.) "Getting out" enables an agent to travel without having to cope with the special attention that customs and border officials often pay to Russians. The agent surrenders his old passport in exchange for the new. When his journey is completed, he makes the exchange again. According to visa stamps, he has spent the entire period in Germany.

AVANPOST

KGB term for a foreign spy cell involving two or more networks. KGB operational procedures would dictate that there be no overlap between the networks, for security reasons.

b

BABBLER

An electronic device that emits what appears to be simultaneous gibberish in at least a dozen languages, used as a counterbugging measure.

BACKSTOPPING

An array of bogus cover identifications issued to an operative that will stand up to fairly rigorous investigation. An agent who is backstopped is first given a birth certificate (either contrived or that of a dead person); then he proceeds to obtain the myriad identification certificates required in a modern society—from Social Security card through driver's license and credit cards to library cards and voter registration. These cards are "real" in the sense that the issuing agency thinks they are being given to a real person. A backstopped agent also has a phone number and mailing address that are "covered" by someone who can pass as a legitimate business or personal associate. Full backstopping is so expensive and time-consuming a process that CIA tries to avoid it in favor of "flash-alias" documentation. This type of documentation consists of counterfeits produced by the Identification Section of Technical Services Division. Technicians there are able to manufacture seemingly legitimate papers ranging from an American Express card to a Libyan driver's license. (As flash-alias credit cards are not real, an agent carrying one uses it only for identification; he must pay cash for meals and hotels.)

BARGAINING COUNTER

An arrested agent who is stored in prison until the proper time arises to barter him for the release of a jailed operative from one's own side.

BARIUM

KGB term for false information that is fed to a suspected source of leaks of classified material. As is true for the barium solution used in gastrointestinal examinations, the course of the "barium material" is watched as it flows toward Western intelligence. Different "doses" of information are given to different officials; the dose that is detected in the West means the end of the spying career of the person who transmitted it.

BAZAAR INTELLIGENCE

Marketplace rumors and gossip, generally with about as much credence as the source would imply. But bazaar intelligence is not to be dismissed out of hand: if prices of basic commodities suddenly soar, the first signs of serious popular discontent will be detected among shoppers.

"A BETTER WORLD," "A WORLD ALL FULL OF BLISS"

Israeli euphemisms for the destination of murdered enemy agents. Similarly, to "send a person on vacation" means to injure him, but nonfatally; the extent of the injury depends on whether the vacation is to be "brief" or "long."

BfV (Bundesamt für Verfassungsschutz)

Federal Office for the Protection of the Constitution, the West German counterintelligence agency. Functions of *BfV* roughly parallel those of the FBI.

BIGOT LIST

A listing of the names of all persons privy to the workings of a particularly sensitive intelligence mission. The bigot list is intended to maintain tight control of the circulation of secret documents, to insure that everyone reading them has a true "need to know."

The term began in World War II, when officers being sent to Gibraltar in preparation for the invasion of North Africa had their orders stamped "TO GIB." Later, when planning commenced for Operation OVERLORD, the Normandy invasion, the letters were reversed to read "BIGOT" and used to list persons with a need-to-know sensitive details of the invasion. *(See also* WITTING.)

BIOGRAPHIC LEVERAGE

CIA euphemism for blackmail—literally, the use of known derogatory information from a person's past that is used to coerce him or her into doing the Agency's bidding.

THE BIRD

See FORT HOLABIRD. CIC.

BIRDWATCHER

A slang word for a spy used by some British intelligence officers in the 1950s. An officer with a penchant for bird-hunting contrived a sublanguage for his subordinates. A birdwatcher who went into the field, for whatever purpose, was called a "poacher," and he was controlled by a "gamekeeper." The target was the "bag." The assistants were "beaters," who flushed the quarry, and "stalkers," who tailed it once it was running.

BLACK BAG JOB

An FBI term for warrantless surreptitious entries for purposes other than microphone installations; i.e., physical search and photographing or seizing documents. The FBI realized it was breaking the law with such raids. As an internal memorandum stated in July 1966, "Such a technique involves trespassing and is clearly illegal; therefore, it would be impossible to obtain any legal sanction for it. Despite this, 'black bag' jobs have been used because they represent an invaluable technique in combating subversive activities of a clandestine nature aimed directly at undermining and destroying our nation." Targets (there were hundreds) ranged from the Ku Klux Klan to Socialist groups. Director J. Edgar Hoover finally ordered the black bag jobs halted in 1966, apparently because of fear of exposure. Numerous Bureau memoranda given the Church Committee warned of FBI embarrassment should the illegal break-ins be revealed. (Also called "surreptitious entry.")

BLACK BAG OPERATION

In CIA terms, an under-the-table operation such as passing funds to a foreign political party.

BLACK BOXES

Inanimate technical methods of spying, ranging from room bugs and telephone taps to satellite reconnaissance.

BLACK FORGERY

Material that is produced so that it appears to be of enemy origin.

BLACK PROPAGANDA

Operations in which the source of the disseminated propaganda is shielded or misrepresented so that it cannot be attributed to the source responsible for it. During World War II, for instance, German intelligence sent letters to French soldiers, purporting to be from hometown neighbors, claiming their wives were committing open adultery or had venereal diseases. Black propaganda is an activity that has now fallen under another umbrella term, "disinformation."

CIA officer E. Howard Hunt did a casebook black propaganda stunt while in the Mexico City station. Hunt learned that a Communist front group planned a reception honoring a Soviet visitor. He obtained an invitation, had a printer run off 3,000 copies, and distributed them all over Mexico City. Since the invitation offered free drinks and a luncheon, the response was so massive that refreshments were swiftly exhausted, and the Communist hosts had to bar the doors, to the outrage of the "invitees" waiting outside. Both the Mexicans and the Soviets went away with sour feelings about one another.

BLACKMAIL

The use of derogatory information to compel a person to work for an enemy intelligence service. Blackmailers have run the gamut of human frailties. One example from among hundreds:

Alfred Frenzel, a member of the West German *Bundestag,* or Parliament, had been a member of the Communist Party in prewar Czechoslovakia, but thought he had thrown off this past by claiming an exemplary war record. He boasted of being a pilot among exiles fighting the Germans for the British, whereas he actually served as a cook. (So firm was Frenzel in details of his story that he won a libel suit against a political opponent who accused him of embroidering his record.) But the Czech secret service knew better, and blackmailed Frenzel into passing along top-secret NATO annual planning reports. He was sentenced to fifteen years' hard labor for espionage in 1961; then he was swapped for a woman journalist arrested by the USSR on trumped-up charges in 1966.

BLACK TRAINEES

Foreigners brought to the United States for training at Camp Peary or another CIA facility, and who are not made aware that they are in the United States.

BLIND DATING

An agreement by an intelligence officer to meet another person at a place of that person's choice. The greatest risk is that the officer can be kidnapped by the other side. The recommended procedure is that a first meeting be held at a relatively public place, such as a square, business district, or park, where neither party can be jeopardized.

BLIND MEMORANDUM

A memorandum written on blank (i.e., no letterhead) stationery with no signature or indication of origin. Intelligence agencies frequently use the blind memorandum as a means of making an informal record, yet without assigning any individual responsibility for its content. Since such memoranda do not contain a file number, they can be destroyed with impunity in the event of threatened disclosure.

BLOWN AGENT

An intelligence operative whose identity becomes known to the opposition. "Blown" also is used to refer to any aspect of an operation whose security has been compromised, be it a safe house, a secret radio frequency, or a letter-drop.

BLOWN BACK

False propaganda planted in a foreign country that is picked up by news organizations and reprinted as fact—or a semblance thereof—by newspapers in the nation of origin. William Colby, one-time director of Central Intelligence, told the Church Committee in 1977 that material the CIA distributed abroad was often "blown back" into the United States as the truth. Although Colby did not deign to say so, American media could avoid blown back news by doing their own reporting, rather than repeating what is reported abroad.

BnD (Bundesnarchrichtendienst)

The West German Federal Intelligence Service concerned both with foreign and domestic intelligence. Successor to the Gehlen Organization; created by CIA, although now feistily independent.

BOFFIN

Communications technician (British).

BOLSHOY CHIREY

Russian for "big boils," an internal KGB epithet for senior officers, whose tempers and pressures are such that they are apt to "burst at any moment."

BOOK MESSAGE

A CIA message that goes to each station and installation in the world. A book message announces personnel changes of general interest and declarations of policy.

BORDER CROSSERS

Agents who attempt to sneak across the border separating Western Europe from the Soviet-bloc countries. CIA wasted much time—and many European-born agents—with border crossings in the late 1940s and early 1950s. The few agents who managed to get past the border guards seldom were able to send back any information of value. Border crossers are now found primarily in blood-and-thunder spy novels. *(See also LINECROSSERS.)*

BOUGHT A DOG

The recruitment, by a case officer, of a "worthless agent, a fabricator, or a con man," according to William Hood, formerly of the CIA.

BOYEVAYA GRUPPA

"Combat gangs," KGB squads trained—and authorized—to kill or abduct targets abroad, as required. *(See also* WET SQUAD.)

BRAINWASHING

A term that came into wide use—or misuse—during the Korean War as descriptive of changes Chinese Communist interrogators made in prisoners' minds through psychological manipulation, physical mistreatment, and drugs. The word suggests Oriental cunning and offered an "answer" as to why many American POWs decided to sign anti-U.S. manifestoes on such subjects as germ warfare and war guilt. But Colonel Allison Ind, who spent much of his Army career as an intelligence officer in the Far East, rejects such colorful interpretations, saying they belong to thriller writers. "What we call brainwashing is quite simply sales psychology driven to its absolute limits in conjunction with an atmosphere which increases receptivity: isolation, doubt as to one's own people, apparent sincerity on the part of the operator." The Dutch-born psychiatrist Dr. Joost A. M. Meerloo uses yet another term, "menticide," or "murder of the mind."

BRIDE

The decoding, by the United States and British intelligence, of thousands of wartime Soviet messages to agents stationed abroad. The highly secret operation began in 1945 and was possible because of the discovery of a partially burned Soviet code book in Finland during the last days of World War II. The decoded messages revealed deep Soviet penetration of the British and U.S. intelligence services, and also gave information on such famed espionage figures as the Rosenbergs, executed in 1953 for wartime atomic espionage. Only the barest hints of Operation Bride's findings have become public. One longtime Western counterintelligence specialist told me, "The full story

would knock the globe off its axis by three degrees." Bride
began as Operation Verona.

BRIGADE 2506

The anti-Castro invasion force in the 1961 Bay of Pigs Operation. Each Cuban freedom fighter who came to the CIA-spon-
sored training base in Guatemala was assigned a number, commencing with 2000. Soldier 2506 fell to his death in a mountain
training accident; his friends honored him by using his number
for the name of their brigade.

BROTHERLY ORGANIZATIONS

Ostensibly independent cultural and political groups in a target country that give aid and comfort to the Soviet Union.
(KGB term.)

BUCKET JOB

When the New York field office of the FBI began trailing Nazi
spies around the city in the 1930s, members of surveillance
teams worked such long and irregular hours that agents joked
about "bringing dinner to work in a bucket." The teams eventually took on the name "bucket squads," and their surveillances came to be known as bucket jobs. An agent working on a
surveillance is "in the bucket," or "carrying the bucket."

BUG

The wiring of a room so that any sound made therein can be
heard and recorded.

Because of tight controls on movements of foreigners, Communist-bloc intelligence services can practically insure continuous electronic "coverage" of targets. According to the defected
Czech agent Josef Frolik, "A number of Prague restaurants—the
better ones—are permanently equipped with audio devices at
certain tables. Waiters in such establishments are trained to recognize persons of interest from photographs. In the event such
a person comes to the establishment, the waiter will seat him at
one of the tables equipped with a monitoring device; such tables are usually marked as having been 'reserved.' " The waiter
announces the other party has cancelled, and after seating the
targets, he goes to the telephone and alerts the "hotel detail" of

the intelligence service, which activates the monitor by remote control. As Frolik notes, "Any kind of checking which a CIA officer may have engaged in prior to meeting a contact or an agent thus [becomes] useless. Because he entered the restaurant at random and did not discuss the location beforehand with his contact or agent, just let an analyst try to find out where a mistake had occurred or at which point the operation was blown."

Counterintelligence specialists responsible for finding and dismantling bugs are aptly called "exterminators."

BUREAU CENTRAL DES RENSEIGNEMENTS ET D'ACTION (BCRA)

A French Resistance organization that combined intelligence-gathering with sabotage during World War II; it worked closely with the British SOE and the American OSS. The exiled General Charles de Gaulle chose Andre Dewavrin to build and then direct BCRA.

BUREAU SPECIAL

An FBI investigation carried on outside the framework of usual Bureau procedures, with no files or records being maintained. Bureau specials generally involve illegal or politically sensitive affairs—for instance, the wiretaps installed on numerous Washington journalists and National Security Council officials by White House order in 1971.

BURN

An intelligence agent who is deliberately sacrificed in order to protect a more valuable and productive spy. British counterintelligence has long suspected (but never conclusively shown) that two prominent Soviet agents were burned to preserve other spies: Klaus Fuchs, of nuclear secrets infamy and John Vassall, an Admiralty functionary forced to spy for the Soviets after being photographed in a homosexual orgy. The British theory was that Fuchs and Vassall were put into positions where they were to be detected, thereby halting searches for other spies in the areas where they worked.

C

CABLE VETTING

British euphemism for a procedure whereby security agencies would routinely scrutinize private cables and telegrams dispatched from or received in the United Kingdom via the post office (which runs the British telegraph system) or private cable companies. The practice was authorized under the Official Secrets Act of 1920 and continued until exposed by the *Daily Express* in February 1967.

CAMP 020

A highly secret interrogation center British intelligence (MI5) utilized to interrogate and confine suspected German agents during World War II. Camp 020 was at Latchmere House, a rambling Victorian mansion amid acres of dense woodland near the Surrey village of Ham Common, originally bought by the War Office as a hospital and recuperation center for officers shell-shocked during World War I. Prisoners taken to Camp 020 effectively disappeared for the duration of the war: the British omitted it from the lists of POW camps given to the International Red Cross for neutral inspection. (Likewise, the Germans did not list their interrogation centers with the IRC.)

Interrogators at Camp 020 relied upon a variety of psychological and other techniques to break prisoners. Under the "soft" approach, a prisoner would be treated with cocktail-party hospitality during which interrogators would reveal what they already knew about the agent and his mission and German intelligence in general. Occasionally German agents already "doubled" would appear and urge the new captive to tell what he knew. In the "hard" approach, the agent would be thrust into solitary confinement, his only contact with the outside being a guard who (for example) might casually comment: "This cell is empty because we shot the previous fellow last night. Have you been told when you are scheduled for the firing squad?" Unconfirmable stories abound about dummy firing squads and torture. According to MI5 historian Nigel West, some German prisoners suffered breakdowns and attempted suicide; only one, however, died in Camp 020—an elderly German who suffered a heart attack during an air raid.

CAMP PEARY

The CIA training facility on a narrow neck of land between the James and York rivers near Williamsburg, Virginia. A Seabee (navy construction battalion) training camp during World War II, Peary passed to CIA in the early 1950s. It then consisted of ramshackle wooden barracks and administrative buildings; by the 1960s red brick buildings gave it the appearance of a small New England college. In its early days, Peary was known as "Camp Swampy"—the terrain had much brackish water—and carried the official cryptonym ISOLATION. (CIA's Office of Training had the misconception that the location and purpose of the facility were deep secrets.) Agency people called Peary "The Farm."

CASE-DEATH

An intelligence operation that fails for no discernible reason. The immediate suspicion is a security breach.

CASE OFFICER

In CIA usage, the person in charge of agents who collect intelligence and perform other clandestine duties. He is the key figure in CIA's Clandestine Service—the "ultimate link between the giant bureaucracy in Washington and the information it wants to collect, and the actions it wants to see taken," as former case officer Joseph Burkholder Smith has written. Contrary to the field agent, the case officer has no direct contact with the opposition. He is responsible for keeping the operation on course, and supplying the agent with the necessary resources (monetary and otherwise) to carry it out.

Under ideal circumstances, the agent's only contact with the intelligence agency is through the case officer. Involving other persons dilutes the case officer's necessary authority and gives the agent a chance for second-guessing. A "horrible example" cited in CIA case studies was the Bay of Pigs. Although Richard Bissell, then the CIA deputy director, was primary case officer, the Cuban exiles with whom he worked—and whom he supposedly controlled—also had access to Adolf Berle, Jr., a State Department official, and Arthur M. Schlesinger, Jr., of the White House staff. This diffused authority was one of many weaknesses that caused the operation to fail.

CASSEROLE
Informer; a French intelligence term.

CATTLE GUARDS
Euphemism for the paramilitary soldiers of fortune hired for antiterrorist operations by the government of South Africa. Ostensibly recruited to protect herds on outlying South African farms, the cattle guards in fact go as far north as Angola in quest of black "terrs" who with outside support are attempting to overthrow the government. As of mid-1984, the pay was $600 to $900 per month, plus room and board and round trip air fare from Europe to Johannesburg.

CAUTERIZATION
Removing compromised agents to safety. CIA had to "cauterize" scores of agents, contract employees, and informants in Mexico, Ecuador, and Uruguay when turncoat officer Phillip Agee of the agency's Western Hemisphere Division revealed their identities in his 1974 book, *Inside the Company: CIA Diary*. The process also involved terminating every operation of which Agee might have knowledge. Agee's mischief cost the United States government uncountable millions of dollars.

CENTER, THE
KGB term for headquarters at 2 Dzerzhinsky Square in Moscow. Also called "Moscow Center."

CHAMFERING
A technique for opening sealed mail—essentially, a sophisticated version of a kitchen tea kettle but designed for mass usage. British intelligence taught the technique to six FBI agents

just before the start of World War II to enable them to open Axis diplomatic mail entering and leaving the United States. Suspended right after the war, the program resumed under CIA sponsorship in the early 1950s. *(See also* FLAPS AND SEALS.)

CHEATERS
Eyeglasses containing thick, clear nonoptical glass, worn to disguise and mask eye movement.

CHEKIST
Member of the *Cheka,* the Soviet secret police founded in 1918 by Felix Dzerzhinsky. The *Cheka* eventually evolved into the present-day KGB, whose agents are still known to many Russians as Chekists (although not out loud).

CHENG PAO K'O
The Chinese counterespionage service used to watch Chinese abroad (both Chinese citizens and the so-called "overseas Chinese") and foreign agents. A separate service, the *Chi Pao K'o,* does internal security.

CHICKEN FEED
The "information" that doubled German agents were permitted to feed back to Berlin during World War II, under control of British intelligence. Chicken feed, while not necessarily inaccurate, was nonetheless inconsequential; it was intended to demonstrate that the German spies were working. Chicken feed was a "mixture of truth, wherever possible," notes Ewen Montagu, a British disinformation officer, "and falsehood where the truth could not be told and where the falsity would not be detected or the detection, when it came, would not matter."

CHIEF OF OUTPOST (COO)
The CIA officer in charge of a field office subordinate to the CIA station in a country.

CHURCH COMMITTEE
The Senate committee that investigated American intelligence during 1975–76. Formally, the Senate Select Committee

to Study Governmental Operations with Respect to Intelligence Activities. The Senate created the committee on January 27, 1975; its final report was issued April 26, 1976. The chairman was Senator Frank Church, Democrat of Idaho.

CHUZHOI

Russian for "alien"; to Soviet intelligence, a person serving a Soviet agency for other than ideological or political reasons. "Usually the term is applied to those who are spies by profession, avocation, or for gain," David J. Dallin notes.

CI-nicks

CIA term for counterintelligence officers of their own organization. Officers in the clandestine service often feel the CI-nicks (pronounced see-niks) gather much information that is never put to operational use.

CLANDESTINE OPERATION

An operation conducted in secrecy, but with no effort to disguise its nature. If a U.S. submarine surfaces off the coast of Iran at night and an agent paddles ashore on a rubber raft, the operation is concealed by natural circumstances, but it is exactly what it appears to be. A cruising patrol boat, or a fisherman, could chance upon the scene and destroy the necessary secrecy. Hence the hazardous nature of clandestine operations. *(See also* COVERT OPERATION.)

CLANDESTINE SERVICES

The portion of the CIA that conducts clandestine operations, synonymous with the Agency's Operations Directorate. By CIA definition, "clandestine" means an activity that is hidden or secret by design.

CLEAN

A piece of intelligence apparatus—an agent, a safe house, a letter-drop, or whatever—that has never been used operationally and hence is unknown to the other side. An astute case officer keeps a stock of clean agents for emergency use; once one is needed, the reason is frequently so urgent there is no time to do the necessary recruiting and security clearance. Such an agent might be used only one time.

COBBLER

KGB term for an intelligence technician who enters false entry and exit stamps in a passport. The term stems from the Soviet habit of calling false passports "shoes." Hence anyone who worked on the shoes was a cobbler.

COCKROACH ALLEY

The cluster of wooden "temporary" buildings on the Mall in Washington that housed CIA's first offices in the late 1940s. Buildings I, J, K, and L shuddered in the slightest breeze, and they smelled; officers walked cautiously over the rotting floors.

COINTELPRO

FBI term for the bureau's "counterintelligence program" of the 1960s and 1970s directed at anti-war and other radical groups, ranging from run-of-the-pulpit pacifists to black militants and white supremacy groups. COINTELPRO utilized a plethora of techniques, ranging from leaking a militant's criminal record to the press to writing spurious letters intended to wreck domestic lives.

Under COINTELPRO, which lasted from 1956 through 1971, techniques the FBI had developed for use against hostile foreign agents were adopted for use against perceived domestic threats to the established political and social order. The Church Committee called COINTELPRO "a sophisticated vigilante operation aimed squarely at preventing the exercise of First Amendment rights of speech and association, on the theory that preventing the growth of dangerous groups and the propagation of dangerous ideas would protect the national security and deter violence."

COLD APPROACH

An attempt to recruit a foreign national as a source without any prior indication that he might be receptive to such an offer. Risky, at the least; disastrous, at the most. A person who rejects a cold approach will report to his government, which will loudly protest the attempt to "bring your Soviet-American clash to our nation." (Also known as a "cold-pitch recruit-ment.")

COMINFIL

An FBI acronym for a 1960s program to counter Communist infiltration of such mass organizations as the NAACP and the scouting movement. The initial technique was to inform a leader of the group about the attempted infiltration and to name the Communist agent. Later, however, the FBI targeted both the Communist infiltrator *and* the organization for embarrassment. For instance, a friendly newsman would be given information about Communist infiltration in a civil rights march, with the express purpose being to discredit both the organizers of the march and the participants. SANE and the United Farm Workers were two early targets.

COMINT

Acronym for "communications intelligence," which in the United States falls under the purview of the National Security Agency (NSA). COMINT is formally defined as "technical and intelligence information derived from foreign communications by other than the intended recipient"; in other words, by intercepting electronic and other communications. (The language is from a National Security Council Intelligence Directive.)

COMMO

CIA's Office of Communications. COMMO provides communications between CIA headquarters and its offices abroad, and "between headquarters and sensitive agents abroad with whom regular contact is impracticable or a threat to their security." Much of this traffic is now via satellite.

COMPANY

Common reference by CIA personnel to their employer. Insiders never use the article "the" when referring to CIA; they simple say the initials. Other euphemisms are "The Agency" or "Langley," the latter the suburban Virginia community in which the CIA's headquarters building is situated.

COMPROMISE

The detection of an agent, a safe house, or an intelligence technique by someone from the other side.

COMPUTERIZED TELEPHONE NUMBER FILE (CTNF)

An FBI file created in 1970 (and since discontinued) that included phone numbers of "black, New Left, and other ethnic extremists."

COMSEC

Acronym for "communications security," the method of protecting communications by providing the means of enciphering messages and by establishing the security of the equipment used to transmit them.

That nations—and intelligence services—now put the most routine of communiques into code has sound historical logic. During the Mexican Revolution, insurgent Francisco (Pancho) Villa happened to capture a federal troop train as he was driving north toward the key city of Juarez. But the five seized cars were not enough to transport his entire army. So Villa had a telegrapher tap out a signal to the federal commander in Juarez: "Engine broken down at Moctezuma. Send another engine and five cars." Villa signed the message in the name of the train commander he had captured. When the "relief train" arrived—and was promptly captured—Villa shot off another bogus message to Juarez stating that a large force of rebels was approaching from the south and asking instructions. The Juarez command ordered him to retreat posthaste. Villa did so, pausing periodically to telegraph cheering messages about the "federal escape." His captured train rolled into Juarez unmolested, and he seized the city virtually without a shot.

CONFIDENTIAL SOURCES

A broad range of persons who supply an intelligence agency with information that is available to them because of their position. The FBI Manual of Instructions, the basic procedural guide for special agents, lists as examples "bankers, telephone company employees, and landlords." CIA's pool of confidential sources includes customs and immigration personnel at international airports. (At the Mexico City airport, for instance, travelers bound for Cuba are routinely photographed for the local CIA station.) Hotel personnel are also valued confidential sources for agencies, as are friendly newspaper writers and editors.

CONSENSUAL ELECTRONIC SURVEILLANCE

Bugging or wiretapping where one party to the conversation consents to the monitoring. The Supreme Court held in 1971 that this type of monitoring does not violate Fourth Amendment rights *(U.S. v. White, 401 US 745)*. Nonetheless, Justice Department guidelines initiated in 1972 require that the attorney general or his designated deputy approve all consensual electronic surveillances conducted by the FBI.

CONTROL

Physical or psychological pressure exerted on an agent or group to insure that the agent or group responds to the direction of an intelligence agency or service.

CONTROL SIGN

A deliberate error of spelling or text used by an agent in communicating with superiors by radio or in writing when he (the agent) has come under hostile intelligence control. (Also called "danger sign.") An example: The agent garbles a word in the text corresponding to the week of the month in which he is transmitting—the second week, the second word; the third week, the third word. Variations are endless.

CO-OPTEES

Soviet diplomatic personnel serving in a foreign embassy who are not KGB officers, but who do the KGB's bidding when ordered.

CORPORATIONS

KGB term for foreign Communist parties, members of which are "corporants."

COUNTERESPIONAGE (CE)

One of the more frequently misunderstood terms in the espionage lexicon. The word "counter" suggests that CE is concerned solely with defending against enemy intelligence operations—finding agents and arresting or otherwise neutralizing them. "Quite to the contrary," notes CIA veteran Christopher Felix, "CE is an offensive operation, a means of obtaining intelligence about the opposition by using—or, more usually, attempting to use—the opposition's operations. CE is a form of secret intelligence operation, but it is a form so esoteric, so complex and important, as to stand by itself."

For a CE operative, the ideal (although rarely achieved) situation would be to winnow his way into the heart of the opposition's ongoing espionage operations: to know what information is being sought, and how and from whom, and what is being found. Through diligence and patience, the CE operative could achieve a position of influence enabling him to control operations against his own country.

The highest form of espionage chess, CE is a blend of wits, intuition, and balance: to maintain his cover, the penetration agent must face the possibility of doing damage to his own agency to maintain credibility. It is not unkind, or inaccurate, to state that CE specialists tend toward paranoia; that the mental juggling required to keep track of double and triple agents, and who has been fed what information for what purpose, is perhaps the most demanding intellectual task of anyone in the business.

The story is told of a CE agent for a Western intelligence organization (not CIA) who reported he had been offered a deputy directorship of the opposition group he had penetrated. "Take it," his chief counseled. "Maybe I should," the CE agent replied, "for I think I've gone about as far as I can in my own organization." He spent the next hour convincing his own chief that he was only joking.

COUNTERGUERRILLA WARFARE

Operations and activities conducted by the armed forces, paramilitary forces, or non-military agencies of a government against guerrillas.

COUNTERINSURGENCY
Military, paramilitary, political, economic, psychological, and civic actions taken by a government to defeat subversive insurgency within a country.

COUNTERINTELLIGENCE
Those actions by an intelligence agency intended to protect its own security and to undermine hostile intelligence operations.

COUNTERINTELLIGENCE CORPS (CIC)
The security police for the United States Army. CIC protects Army installations from intruders of a security nature (the military police worry about vandals; the CIC about spies). CIC is also responsible for security clearances for military personnel in sensitive assignments. Through the mid-1950s, CIC did the bulk of counter-Soviet work in Western Europe, only to be supplanted by CIA. In the 1970s, CIC was incorporated into the Defense Investigative Services, an all-services agency. The Golden Sphinx replicas worn by CIC officers were replaced by a new insignia, a composite of the sun's rays, a rose, and a dagger, symbolizing "the search for information, trustworthiness, and danger." Old CIC people still prefer the Sphinx.

COUNTERRECONNAISSANCE
Measures taken to prevent observation by a hostile foreign service of an area, place, or military force. At its lowest form, counterreconnaissance consists of putting signs outside sensitive government installations prohibiting photography. There is a yarn in intelligence circles, perhaps apocryphal, perhaps not, of an innovative FBI agent who tired of tailing two KBG agents ("legals") around nuclear installations in Tennessee. He "borrowed" a truck and rammed the side of their car, damaging it so badly they had to return to Washington by bus, their mission scrubbed.

COUNTERSURVEILLANCE
The process of insuring that an agent is not being surveilled when he sets out to keep an appointment with a contact. Soviet tradecraft calls for the agents to move about for at least two

hours before the contact, changing from subways to cabs to foot, and traveling in no pre-set pattern. If he suspects he is being followed, he has a variety of options to shake himself free —for instance, darting into a busy department store that has many floors, many elevators, and many exits. If a meeting is especially sensitive, the agent might be trailed by colleagues who will watch for signs of a surveillance. Former CIA Soviet expert Harry Rositzke has called New York City "the best place in the world to slip a surveillance," what with its crowded streets, vast parks, and intricate subway system.

The subject of a surveillance operates at an advantage. Maintaining a round-the-clock watch requires at least twelve agents from the rival service—a manpower investment that is difficult to sustain.

Soviet practice in Washington is to "scatter" upward of two dozen known KGB and GRU operatives from the embassy on Tunlaw Road Northwest within minutes of one another. Some dart for Virginia, others for Maryland, still others drive aimlessly around the District of Columbia. The intention, obvious to FBI surveillance teams, is that one of the agents intends a meeting, and the dilution of the surveillance effort increases the chance for success. The "scatter" moves generally come at dusk, when heavy traffic hampers effective surveillance.

The Czech State Security Service (STB, by its Czech-language initials) has a much-admired (and copied) surveillance system. The unnamed mastermind who drew up the basic system had the Prague street system adjusted—one way streets— so that cars driven by Western diplomats followed predictable routes to and from the center city from their residences or embassies. Czech agents routinely attached homing devices to diplomatic cars.

According to Josef Frolik, who defected to CIA from Czech intelligence, "Surveillance teams utilize all possible camouflage systems. Their vehicles have rotable registration plates, the roofs of vehicles can change color by removing a plastic foil, luggage racks are installed on vehicles or taken off, vehicles can have Austrian, West German or Swiss tags; vehicles marked 'driver school' or 'rescue service' are used; other vehicles have easily removable markings indicating various enterprises and institutions. . . . Individuals conducting surveillance on foot are disguised as villagers, soldiers, mailmen, forestry workers.

. . . Every surveillance team has their clothing in one vehicle where the person . . . can change clothes, or put on his glasses, pick up a suitcase or other pieces of luggage. For a time, use was even made of a 'blind' person with a cane and a seeing-eye dog . . ."

COURIER

A messenger responsible for the secure physical transmission and delivery of documents and material. Even journalists are sometimes so foolish that they will agree to mail a letter abroad for someone who purports to be a friend. Such dupes are afforded the courtesy of being described as "unwitting couriers."

COUSINS

The term British and American intelligence officers use for one another. But to the Israelis, "cousins" has a sharply different meaning. When a Mossad agent refers to a cousin, he means an Arab, a reference to the common Semitic origin of the Israelis and the Arabs, both descended from the patriarch Abraham.

COVER

The role played by an intelligence officer to conceal his true purpose for living or traveling abroad. "The best cover is that which contains the least notional and the maximum possible legitimate material," maintains CIA veteran Christopher Felix. An oft-cited example of nigh-perfect cover was that of Richard Sorge, the Soviet spy who lived in prewar Tokyo in the guise of a German journalist. (The only blank, and one not detected until Sorge's arrest, was his whereabouts the years he was training in Moscow.) Sorge's cover was so good that he managed to work in Tokyo for nine years, gathering reams of intelligence from the German embassy and elsewhere for transmission to Moscow. Poor radio security finally undid Sorge, who was hanged. (Sorge even managed to maintain his cover after a drunken escapade that ended with him crashing a motorcycle into the wall of the American Embassy. Although severely injured, and either in a coma or delirious for several days, Sorge said not a word inconsistent with his cover role.)

British businessman Greville Wynne, a counterintelligence officer during World War II, was given a vague instruction by an old intelligence friend in 1955 that it might be useful if he developed business contacts in Eastern Europe. From 1955 to 1960, Wynne did just that, establishing himself as a commercial traveler and salesman for a number of British industrial plants on trips to a number of Communist-bloc nations, including the USSR. Not until 1960 did Wynne come into direct contact with the agent-in-place he was to handle: Colonel Oleg Penkovskiy, perhaps the most important spy ever to work for Western intelligence. Further, their first contact was at a meeting with Soviet trade officials, which Wynne arranged in the course of building contacts in the USSR; not until later was he informed that the entire operation had been tailored to bring him into seemingly casual contact with Penkovskiy. Wynne's superb—and natural —cover lasted almost two years, until he and Penkovskiy were arrested.

By reliable estimate, Soviet intelligence agents fill 60 to 70 percent of the "diplomatic" slots in USSR embassies in Washington, London, Paris, Tokyo, and Mexico City. New arrivals seldom keep their cover beyond a few weeks; they are "burned" by FBI surveillance and in-place informants in the Soviet Embassy. One story, perhaps apocryphal—but perhaps not—is of the FBI agent detailed to cover a minor American diplomat who had arranged a meeting with a KGB contact in a motel parking lot in suburban Virginia. Another agent reported by radio that the KGB man had been involved in a traffic accident en route, and could not possibly make the rendezvous. But despite the hour, and the cold, wet rain, the American diplomat showed no signs of leaving the parking lot. In shivery frustration, the FBI man finally rapped on his car window and announced, in a borscht-circuit Russian accent, "Boris no come, you go home, he call you maybe tomorrow." Several weeks later, the KGB man and the diplomat were caught in the espionage equivalent of *en flagrante;* one delictor was expelled, the other was debriefed and permitted to resign. The surveilling agent filed a somewhat less than complete report on his penultimate surveillance and was subsequently promoted.

COVER BOY

British jocular term for an American felt to be concealing intelligence activities behind a cover job, governmental or otherwise.

COVER FOR STATUS

As defined by former CIA officer Joseph Burkholder Smith, "an activity that explains by some believable story, other than the truth, why a spy sees the people he does, is surrounded by the accoutrements he possesses, lives the way he does, and so forth . . ." Smith had such cover in Indonesia in the 1950s by posing as a representative of a New York firm that was to create a chain of bookstores. His concurrent "cover for action" was to actually run a bookstore that he could use to meet agents he recruited locally. The projects proved such a financial disaster that CIA dropped them in short order.

COVER NAMES

The pseudonym assigned an agent for security purposes. This name is used in general files, and the person's true identity is recorded only in a tightly secured central security registry. No particular rule is followed in choosing such names, but the British permit themselves occasional whimsy. An agent who worked with the famed Dusko Popov was of such girth that his control officer dubbed him "Balloon." A German agent doubled by the Twenty Committee operation was code-named "Tate" because of his resemblance to Harry Tate, a popular music-hall comedian of the era. Edward Chapman, safecracker-turned-spy, told so many conflicting stories when offering his services to MI5 (as a defecting Abwehr agent) that he was named "Zig-zag."

Soviet tradecraft calls for frequent changes of code-names assigned agents. To confuse Western counterintelligence agencies, male agents often are assigned female code-names and vice versa.

COVER ORGANIZATIONS

Organizations created solely to provide cover for a covert agent (unlike "organizational cover," where an existing, legitimate organization is so used). These organizations can range from the one-man law office of Peter Ward, the fictional agent of many E. Howard Hunt spy novels, to the Gibraltar Steamship Company, a major cover group for the Bay of Pigs invasion. (The Bay of Pigs, indeed, grew so vast that the Agency created a subsidiary of a car-rental agency in Florida so that it would not have to account for the movements of all the vehicles.) Cover organizations have imitated virtually every type of business and private group, from labor unions to newspapers and export-import companies. A main requirement is that the cover organization provide the agent or agents working for it with plausible reasons to travel and keep odd hours. (There can be embarrassments. A CIA officer worked in Mexico in the 1960s under cover provided by a major international cotton trading company. At a party one evening he encountered a German who, during casual conversation, remarked that he was in the "cotton business." The German, however, proved to know nothing about cotton. The CIA man made some quiet inquiries and discovered that the Germans had set up a minor intelligence shop in Mexico City under the guise of a cotton company.)

Cover organizations have a long history. During the American Revolution, the French wished to help the colonists fight the British, but not openly. So at the urging of Pierre Auguste Caron de Beaumarchais, a poet, playwright, and independently wealthy man, the government created a "private" trading firm, Hortalez and Company. Acting through Hortalez, the French government literally opened its doors and arsenals to the revolutionists; by one estimate, 90 percent of the arms used in the Battle of Saratoga came through the company. (Unfortunately, de Beaumarchais had to sue his own government to be reimbursed for his out-of-pocket costs; not until 1835 did the U.S. Congress pay his heirs' last claims.)

An essential rule is that a cover organization have authentic enough underpinnings—say, an office, however so meager, and a listed telephone—that a few routine phone calls won't expose it as a myth. In 1960, two United States students, arrested in the USSR, claimed they were researchers traveling for an "educational fund" in Baltimore. A Baltimore newspaperman sought to locate the fund, with the anticipation that its officials would deny any involvement in espionage. Not a trace of the "fund" could be found. The students spent several months in jail before the Soviets turned them loose. They were, in fact, on a journey that involved low-level espionage.

COVER RULES

In selecting cover for its officers working in enemy territory, the Office of Strategic Services stressed what it termed "The Five Freedoms of Cover," to wit:

- Freedom of Action—What can he do?
- Freedom of Movement—Where can he go?
- Freedom of Leisure—How much time will he have for his "hobby"?
- Social Freedom—What kinds of people can he associate with?
- Financial Freedom—How much money can he spend?

As an OSS training manual stated, "Selection of cover for an agent must be based on two primary considerations: (a) the cover must be safe, and (b) it must provide opportunity for him to fulfill his assignment."

COVER STORY

A plausible explanation employed to explain an operation that goes awry. For instance, the U-2 spy plane shot down over Russia in 1959 was officially explained (at first) as a weather reconnaissance craft. The bitter lesson of U-2 is that the cover story had best not be told until an agency knows exactly what counterinformation is held by the other side. The Russians held not only the wreckage of the U-2, with cameras intact, but also the live pilot, Gary Powers.

COVERT OPERATION

An operation using a cover story to conceal the real purpose of the agent's mission. If the CIA sneaks an agent into Iran under the guise of being a businessman, and he steals away for a few hours to do his business, he is operating covertly. In contrast to a "clandestine" operation, no effort is made to shield a covert operation from view; the agent relies upon his wits to avoid detection. (As summarized by Christopher Felix, formerly of CIA, "In brief, the working distinction between the two forms of secrecy (i.e., clandestine and covert) is that a clandestine operation is hidden, but not disguised, and a covert operation is disguised, but not hidden." *(See also* CLANDESTINE OPERATION.)

Joseph Burkholder Smith, longtime CIA officer turned historian after retirement, cites President James Madison's attempt to wrest Florida away from Spain in 1811 as the United States' first covert action. The same techniques were used time and again in Latin America: "The common pattern it established, from which the others were cut, consisted of a preliminary propaganda phase—working up excitement in and about the target —then the organizing of a 'patriot government' opposed to the group we wished to get rid of, then an armed attack by the 'patriots' on the nearest legitimate authority over which the targeted group held sway, then an appeal to the United States government to assume control and restore 'order,' a call which the United States . . . usually answered."

Historically the United States government has found ways to conceal funding for intelligence and other covert activities. In the Florida operation, for instance, President Madison had Congress appropriate $2 million "to defray any expenses which may be incurred in relation to the intercourse between the United States and foreign nations." Even this euphemistic language was hidden in a secret Presidential message to Congress. The money was intended as a bribe to Napoleon of France to pressure Spain to cede the desired territory. Representative John Randolph of Virginia challenged the President and his men for having Congress "do all the dirty work which would otherwise have soiled their fingers." Randolph failed; Madison got his covert funds. The plan failed, however, when Napoleon refused cooperation.

CREDIT CARD REVOLUTIONARIES

FBI term for the middle- and upper-income persons who gave support to anti-war and leftist groups during the late 1960s and early 1970s. (Actress-activist Jane Fonda, for instance, gave an American Express card to an organizer for Vietnam Veterans Against the War to finance his cross-country travels.)

CRYPTOMATERIAL
All material—including documents, devices, equipment, and apparatus—essential to the encryption, decryption, or authentication of telecommunications.

CRYPTONYM
A false name assigned to a covert agent; also, a cover name for a secret operation. During an operation, an agent is never referred to by his true identity, even in the supposed privacy of a headquarters office. One reason is the ever-present fear of electronic surveillance; another is to accustom case officers to speak of the person by his cover name, so that its use becomes second-nature. For further security, the cryptonym is changed frequently as an operation progresses.

For administrative convenience, CIA cryptonyms—operational code names—use a two-letter digraph at the beginning of the word. The digraph can designate either a geographic location or a general subject matter. During the Korean War, the letters TP indicated activities directed against Communist China. (For example, TP-STOLE was the cover name for an operation involving the hijacking of a Scandinavian freighter carrying medical supplies to the enemy.) During the 1960s, MH indicated matters relating to internal U.S. security. Hence MH-CHAOS came to denote activities directed at anti-war protesters.

CRIME RECORDS DIVISON
The FBI's euphemistically titled public relations arm. The division, in the headquarters division in Washington, is responsible for high-level media contacts. One of the more tightly guarded items in the crime records division was the list of reporters considered to be "friendly media," who wrote pro-FBI stories. At the field office (i.e., local) level, the FBI relied upon what it called "confidential sources"—press friends—both to pass along information to which they were privy as reporters, and to write about the bureau in a friendly fashion.

CRYPTANALYSIS
The breaking of codes and ciphers into plain text without initial knowledge of the key used in the encryption.

CRYPTOGRAPHY

The enciphering of plain text so that it will be unintelligible to an unauthorized recipient.

CRYPTOLOGY

The science that embraces cryptoanalysis and cryptography, and includes communications intelligence and communications security.

CRYPTOSECURITY

That component of communications security that results from the provision of technically sound cryptosystems and their proper use.

CRYPTOSYSTEMS

The associated items of cryptomaterial that are used as a unit and provide a single means of encryption and decryption.

CULTIVATION

The process of establishing rapport with a possible source of information or a potential defector. Cultivation commences with a show of friendship and a tangible offer—say, a dinner or even an all-expenses-paid or discount trip to the foreign country. Soviet "diplomats" in Washington constantly offer such bait to Americans whom they consider of potential value. During the 1960s journalists in Washington who covered national security affairs learned to report "cultivation approaches," such as dinner invitations, to the FBI's Washington field office. A phone call would save them the bother of having an FBI agent come to ask, "What did Counsellor Ivanov talk about at his house when you and your wife were there for dinner the other night?"

CUSTODIAL DETENTION LIST

In the words of FBI Director J. Edgar Hoover in 1940, "a suspect list of individuals whose arrest might be considered necessary in the event the United States becomes involved in war." Hoover had American citizens in mind, as well as aliens. Hoover's list was never used. When Attorney General Francis

Biddle ordered it destroyed in 1943 (claiming the concept was "impractical, unwise and dangerous"), Hoover simply changed the title to "Security Index" and his agents kept adding names to it. The existence of the renamed list, understandably, was a closely guarded secret within the Bureau. Later, the file was known variously as the "Reserve Index" and the "Communist Index." The latter designation indicated the shift in emphasis from coverage of Nazis to Communists. But persons the FBI considered to be active Soviet espionage agents were not listed for fear of security leaks. By 1951, more than 15,000 persons— the bulk of them members of the Communist Party (U.S.A.), plus a handful of Puerto Rican nationalists—were on Hoover's list as prospects for detention in the event of national emergency.

CUSTOMERS

The various government departments that use information and analyses produced by intelligence agencies.

CUT-OUT

The go-between, or link, between separate components of an intelligence organization—for instance, the person who maintains contact with a clandestine agent on behalf of the handler controlling him. The existence of the cut-out makes it unnecessary for the clandestine agent to know the exact identity of persons superior to him in the organization. There are two basic types of cut-out systems:

- In the *block* cut-out, the contact knows the name of each agent working in an individual operation or cell;
- In the *chain* cut-out, the contact knows only one agent; any others are recruited sequentially, with agents knowing only the persons directly above and below him.

The cut-out permits oral contact when direct physical contact or a written communication would be dangerous. The cut-out also enables the case officer's true identity to be concealed from the agent, thereby lessening the danger of exposure. If the KGB arrests an agent working in East Germany, for instance, all he knows is that he received money and instructions from a man named "John" who was speaking on behalf of an unknown person named "Carl." Often the agent is not even certain which intelligence agency employs him (other than that is it Western or Soviet-bloc).

d

D-NOTICE, DEFENSE-NOTICE

A British system for "voluntary"—but enforceable—censorship of the press. The Defense-Notice is a formal letter circulated confidentially to mass media editors warning that certain information should remain secret. The information is usually material protected by Britain's Official Secrets Act and which is in danger of disclosure. The D-Notice is issued by authority of something called the "Services, Press and Broadcasting Committee," composed of four government and eleven press representatives. A D-Notice normally originates with a government agency such as MI5 or MI6 that fears one of its secrets is about to be published. It is circulated to committee members and then issued under the name of the secretary, a permanent civil servant. In emergencies, the secretary can issue a D-Notice on his own authority. The secretary is also available to offer "guidance" at all hours on whether particular information should be published. A D-Notice can remain in effect for a specified period of time or indefinitely.

The D-Notice itself is considered a confidential document. But some examples have leaked over the years. In 1967, the *Spectator* published two D-Notices dating to the 1950s. One asked the media to make no references to "secret intelligence or counter-intelligence methods and activities in or outside the United Kingdom." Included were any references whatsoever to the identity or numbers of intelligence personnel or the organizations they served or their bases, recruiting, or training. Another D-Notice—a "standing request"—asked newspapers to make no reference to "cyphering work carried out in Government communications establishments . . . [or] to the fact that on occasions it is necessary in the interest of defense for the services to intercept such communications."

British intelligence has also used D-Notices to prevent trade embarrassment. When George Blake went on trial as a Soviet spy in 1961, a D-Notice asked that editors not reveal he had worked for MI6 as well as the GRU.

DAJNAVNA SIGURNOST (DS)

Bulgarian secret police directly controlled by the KGB. The subservient *DS* draws such high-risk assignments as the attempted assassination of Pope John Paul II. *DS* is headquartered at 30 General Gurko Street, Sofia.

DAMAGE CONTROL

The means by which an intelligence organization attempts to minimize the harmful results of an operation that aborts. The agency must learn as rapidly—and accurately—as possible exactly what agents and facilities might have been compromised to the other side, and thus lost.

One index of an agent's toughness is his ability to pass back to his control the exact information he has given under interrogation. Heinz Felfe, acting head of the Gehlen Organization's counterintelligence department, was arrested in 1961 and convicted of being a Soviet double agent for at least a decade. Since most of his work for Gehlen had dealt with Soviet affairs, both sides had a keen interest in knowing (a) what he had done and (b) what he had told. Felfe said little under interrogation. While in Karlsruehe, the West German prison for top-security prisoners, he managed to send to the Soviets a précis of his "confession"—what his interrogators had asked, and how he had responded. (Questions often indicate the amount of independent information an intelligence agency has concerning a suspect and his ring.) Felfe smuggled his reports from prison via bales of the German popular magazines *Freundin* (The Girl Friend) and *Film Revue,* which were addressed to subscribers by prisoners under contract. Other messages went to his mother in East Germany in secret ink writing.

The mischief—a weak word; call it *disaster*—of a traitor was illustrated during the 1960s espionage trial of Hans Clemens, a turncoat counterintelligence official in the Gehlen Organization. The judge asked Clemens, "Did you tell the Russians where the *BnD* [the West German intelligence organization] has its espionage schools?"

Clemens smiled broadly and replied, "You mean *had* their espionage schools."

The judge, unmoved by the levity, stated during sentencing, "Codes had to be altered, agents exchanged, old and tried contacts severed, live- and dead-letter boxes abandoned, couriers and courier routes altered. Much of eleven years of development work had to be scrapped."

DAME

Acronym for a course entitled "Defense Against Methods of Entry," taught at the Army Intelligence School, Fort Holabird, Maryland, during the 1950s. Of the three-week course, two weeks and four-and-one-half days were devoted to teaching fledgling agents how to pick locks and break into safes. As a sort of afterthought, the last afternoon of the three weeks concerned defense methods against lockpickers. Persons who completed the course were never concerned about losing their car or locker keys—each was given a set of sophisticated picks upon graduation. *(See also* LOCK STUDIES.)

DANGER SIGN

See CONTROL SIGN.

DANGLE

A person who approaches an intelligence agency in such a manner that he is asking to be recruited as an agent to spy against his own country.

Harry Rositzke, long a Soviet specialist for CIA, has written, "The worst mistake any service can make is to recruit as an agent a man who has been 'dangled' before it by a hostile service. The basic rule of thumb in the business of recruiting is to suspect anyone who takes the initiative in making contact with an intelligence officer."

A KGB manual warns its U.S.-based operatives against FBI attempts to dangle supposed recruits. It notes that "the person being dangled either attempts to interest us in his intelligence potential or he takes the initiative and offers to pass us certain secret materials." Such dangles "display a disproportionate interest in money . . ." KGB also cautioned against "persons with liberal views who have contacts with Soviet installations."

DASE

Acronym for a course entitled "Defense Against Sound Equipment," taught at the Army Intelligence School during the 1950s. As was true of the DAME course at the same school (see above), most of the instruction involved methods of bugging rooms and tapping phones, with defensive techniques taught in by-the-way fashion. Some of the techniques taught at Holabird in 1956 were revealed as "dazzling new technology" during Senate investigations of private investigators of the 1960s. One rule of thumb in bugging is that any method discussed in the press is already outdated.

DEAD DROP BOX, DEAD-LETTER DROP

A location where a message can be concealed by an agent for retrieval by another party.

The system devised for Colonel Oleg Penkovskiy seemed superfluously elaborate. He would first paint a black mark on a certain street post, then put his communication in the designated hiding place (one used was a space behind a radiator in a lobby between a butcher shop and a shoe store); next, telephone two Moscow numbers and, when a person answered, hang up. A former intelligence officer says, to the contrary, the phone calls were necessary: Penkovskiy might be detected painting the spot on the post, and depositing the letter. The phone calls were the extra security, for without them no British intelligence agent would pick up the dead drop letter. *(See also* DUBOK, LETTER-DROP.)

DECEPTION

"Luring your opponent into doing voluntarily and by choice what you want him to do," in the words of Christopher Felix. The most historically significant example was the "bodyguard of lies" (Churchill's phrase) the Allies posted around the Normandy invasion of June 1944—first, to convince the Germans that the landing would take place elsewhere; second, that the first landing was a diversion, and that the main strike would come days later, to the north.

DECRYPT

To convert encrypted text into plain text by use of a cryptosystem.

DEE-SID

See DIRECTOR OF CENTRAL INTELLIGENCE DIRECTIVE.

DEFECTOR

A person who, for political or other reasons, has repudiated his country and who may be in possession of information of interest to an enemy government.

Handling of a potential defector is one of the more demanding tasks of intelligence. Agents must first establish that the defector is not a "plant" sent over by the rival service. Then an attempt must be made to persuade the defector to "stay in place"—that is, keep his old job in his country—and pass along current information, with the promise of being given asylum in due course. Given the psychic traumas of defection, convincing a person to stay in his country as an active spy is a strong challenge. It can work: The CIA convinced Soviet Colonel Oleg Penkovskiy, for instance, to continue working in a high military position for almost two years after he announced his willingness to defect. More often than not, the defector refuses and demands asylum.

Neither the United States nor any other Western country automatically "opens the door" to a volunteer defector. Expense is one factor, for defectors must be subjected to lengthy debriefing, and then be "relocated" under a new name and given a living subsidy for a period of several years. A former CIA official who worked in three Western European stations states, "If you've already spent hundreds of thousands of dollars—and years of man-hours—on a guy who walked in from the Soviet air ministry, what do you say when a guy from the desk next to his shows up? Is he worth the investment?" Rank is one determinant. Any Soviet or bloc military figure of the rank of colonel or above apparently is accepted without question; majors and captains would be required to produce evidence they could be of intelligence value. A KGB or GRU agent of any level is given sanctuary (although they can expect prolonged isolation and interrogation under drugs, as a necessary means of establishing their bona fides).

The Soviets routinely cover up high-level defections by putting out stories to the effect that "Colonel General X" died in a plane crash, rather than admit he fled to the United States or Great Britain. British intelligence and CIA produced no less than twenty "dead Russian officers" in the flesh in 1961 to convince Colonel Oleg Penkovskiy that many of his trusted past colleagues had cast their lot with the West and had survived and flourished. Western intelligence publicizes only a minute fraction of the defectors who come across in any given year: thus the KGB is seldom *absolutely* certain of the whereabouts of an officer who disappears.

If the West decides to "surface" a defector and publicize the fact he has "come over," and hint at the value of the information he carried, the Soviets respond with character assassination. Their press depicts the defector as a man who stole money, abused his family, had psychological problems, or whatnot. The author unwittingly accepted such "disinformation" as truth in writing about an Eastern-bloc military defector in the 1960s. An Eastern European diplomat gave me such a deliciously salacious—and convincing—account of the "real reason" the man defected that I published it. CIA friends quickly told me I had been hoodwinked. I saw the maligned man at a social function years later, but did not have the nerve to apologize. I was told he dismissed the story as "a tribute to my virility which I truly do not deserve."

DEFENSE INTELLIGENCE AGENCY (DIA)

The Department of Defense agency responsible for producing military intelligence for the four services. Secretary of Defense Robert S. McNamara created DIA in 1961 in an attempt to produce a coordinated intelligence effort by the services, rather than the bifurcated reports and estimates he saw during his first months in the Pentagon. DIA worked better than most intelligence professionals expected; it now has a budget and a bureaucracy (partly civilian) rivaling that of CIA.

DEFENSE INTELLIGENCE OBJECTIVES AND PRIORITIES (DIOP)

A single statement of intelligence requirements compiled by DIA for use by all Department of Defense intelligence activities. The DIOP, in effect, is the "master shopping list" for American military intelligence. Because it tells what the Pentagon *needs,* rather than *knows,* a DIOP is a closely held document.

DEMORALIZATION

A means by which KGB salvages some good from a failed operation. As defined by former American intelligence officer Edward Van Der Rhoer, "When an operation has outlived its usefulness or has finally been exposed, the KGB seeks to terminate it in such a way that maximum demoralization occurs on the other side, with accompanying loss of confidence of people in their government. If citizens at large believe that their government is infiltrated at many levels, if they find their leaders incompetent or venal, national stability is bound to be adversely affected." Van Der Rhoer cited as an example the Soviet gloating over the disclosure that a key aide to Chancellor Willy Brandt of West Germany was an agent of East German intelligence, a KGB surrogate. The loss of the agent was a blow to KGB—but in retribution, it so shattered public confidence in Brandt that he was forced out of office in 1974. A continuing demoralization campaign concerns the Philby-Burgess-Maclean spy ring, which seems to reappear in the British press every two years with cyclic regularity.

DENIABILITY

The deliberate use of euphemisms that gives the President of the United States (or another high official) grounds for denying knowledge of covert activities discussed at a meeting that he attended. (I use the United States because the Soviet leadership, with its controlled press, does not have to bother with explanations of *any* of its activities because the public knows nothing other than what it is told.) During 1960, for instance, President Eisenhower spoke so strongly about Patrice Lumumba, an erratic Congolese rebel, that Robert Johnson of the National Security Council staff heard his words as "an order for [Lumumba's] assassination." But when he wrote minutes of the meeting, he carefully excised any mention of Eisenhower's statement. CIA, meanwhile, proceeded with an assassination plan. (Lumumba meanwhile was killed by rivals acting independently of CIA.)

Given the veiled language employed when persons have "deniability" in mind, William Colby, the former director of Central Intelligence, has written that matters can easily go beyond desired bounds: ". . . [In] the macho atmosphere of secret operations, a substratum of the violently inclined will always tend to discount normal moral restraints or exceed their original instructions in the heat of action, and any encouragement from above can launch them into horrendous behavior, and once launched, they are difficult to recall or control."

In discussing "deniability," intelligence officers hark back to Henry II's query about Thomas à Becket: "Who will free me from this turbulent priest?" The cleric shortly thereafter was killed in Canterbury Cathedral. But: did the king actually *order* the murder? Or did his courtiers put their own interpretation on his outburst?

DENIED AREA

A country with such strict internal security that foreign intelligence agents dare not contact informants in person. By CIA definition, this includes the Soviet Union, Cuba, and (to a lessening degree) the People's Republic of China. In a denied area, agents rely upon dead drops and clandestine radios to maintain contact and to pass information.

DEPARTMENTAL INTELLIGENCE

The intelligence that U.S. government departments and agencies generate in support of their own activities. Such intelligence is not routinely shared. For instance, the FBI might run across information of value to the Drug Enforcement Administration. Rather than forward it in comradely fashion (both agencies *do* work for the same government), the FBI would be apt to barter and elicit information of equal value from DEA.

DESTABILIZATION

The process of undermining, to the point of collapse, a foreign government through overt political and economic actions.

Although the term is said to be of CIA origin, as descriptive of
the efforts to overthrow President Salvatore Allende of Chile in
the early 1970s, former CIA officer David Atlee Phillips attributes its first use—and subsequent introduction into the American political lexicon—to Representative Michael Harrington, a
Massachusetts Democrat and a vocal critic of the agency. Harry
Shlaudeman, formerly number-two man in the embassy in
Chile, had been questioned by Harrington during Congressional hearings in April 1974. Shlaudeman then telephoned
Phillips, CIA's chief of Latin American operations, and asked
him: "He [Harrington] kept asking me about the 'destabilization' of the Allende regime. Have you people given Congress
anything to indicate that 'destabilizing' was the plan?" Phillips
assured Shlaudeman he had never heard of the word. Proceed-
ings of the hearings (before the Latin American subcommittee
of the House Foreign Affairs Committee) show that Harrington
used the word "destabilization" three times before attributing it
to William Colby, the director of Central Intelligence. Despite
this history, "There is nothing that will change the current usage of 'destabilization,' " Phillips recognized in his memoir.

DETERRENT TAIL
Watchers who deliberately let their quarry know they are
being followed to scare them out of achieving their purpose.

DEVELOP
To cultivate a sympathizer into becoming an active espionage
agent, generally on ideological grounds.

D.G.S.E.
See S.D.E.C.E.

DIRECCION GENERAL DE LA INTELIGENCIA (DGI)
Cuba's intelligence service, organized and directed by Eastern
European Bloc services, particularly the East Germans. DGI
does surrogate work for the Soviet KGB throughout the world.
Its United States outpost is run through the Cuban Mission to
the United Nations in New York with a strong substation based
in the Cuban Interests Section of the Czech embassy in Wash-

ington. As is true of other Communist Bloc nations, DGI is
slavishly subservient to KGB.

DIRECTOR OF CENTRAL INTELLIGENCE DIRECTIVE (DCID, OR DEE-SID)

A directive issued by the director of Central Intelligence that
outlines general policies and procedures to be followed by intelligence agencies under his direction. A dee-sid is generally
more specific than a National Security Council Intelligence Directive ("nee-sid").

DIRECTORATE "S"

The KGB wing responsible for directing the work of "illegals" abroad.

DIRTY TRICKS, CZECH STYLE

In 1962 a West German tank regiment arrived in Wales, Great
Britain, for training in NATO exercises. Alarmed at the growing
military cooperation between West Germany and the United
Kingdom, the KGB, through its Czech subsidiary, decided to
create the public impression that the German soldiers were
anti-Semitic Nazis. The Czech agent stationed in Wales received
orders to paint swastikas on Jewish graves and vandalize Jewish
graveyards. The British press accused the Germans of responsibility for these ghoulish acts.

DISCARD

An agent betrayed by his own service in order to protect
another, more valuable, source of information.

DISINFORMATION (dezinformatsiya)

A KGB term denoting a variety of techniques and activities
to purvey false or misleading information, including rumors,
insinuation, and altered facts. CIA cited numerous case histo-
ries in a 1982 report on Soviet active measures, ranging from
the spread of a rumor that the United States was behind the
seizure of the Grand Mosque in Mecca in the late 1970s, to
forged "top secret" documents showing that the United States
intended to use nuclear weapons against the territory of its

NATO allies. Disinformation is a key element of Soviet "active measures."

DISPATCHED AGENT

An operative who seeks out a rival intelligence agency and claims he wishes to defect, when in actuality he is attempting a penetration. If the operative arouses suspicions, he is subjected to intense and prolonged interrogation. One such suspect was Yuri Nosenko, a former KGB officer who in 1964 appeared at a CIA office abroad with a claim that he had "handled" Lee Harvey Oswald when the Presidential assassin resided in the Soviet Union. Although Oswald himself, at the U.S. embassy in Moscow, confessed having told the Soviets everything classified he had learned during his years in the Marine Corps, Nosenko insisted that Oswald in fact had not even been interrogated. The CIA counterintelligence section refused to believe such an unlikely claim, and so from April 1964 to December 1968 Nosenko was held in solitary confinement and subjected to devious psychological pressures. CIA finally concluded that he was a bona fide defector.

Nosenko has since been given a new identity and a position as a CIA "consultant." Many persons within the Agency continue to entertain doubts about his authenticity, asserting the KGB "sent him over" to persuade the U.S. government that the Soviet Union had no role in the Kennedy murder.

DISPOSAL

CIA term for the dismissal of a non-career agent, usually a non-American who has worked for American intelligence for diverse reasons. (Christopher Felix of the Agency thought the term "unnecessarily macabre.") Disposal can be done either directly—the case officer or the cut-out tells the agent his services are no longer required; or indirectly—the case officer simply breaks off contact without saying a word; or maliciously—the case officer uses Agency facilities to tarnish the reputation of the ousted agent or arranges for his arrest on either real or contrived charges. No firm rules govern disposals, for each agent is different. *(See also* TERMINATE WITH EXTREME PREJUDICE, EXECUTIVE ACTION.)

DISSEMINATION

The distribution of information or intelligence products in written, oral, or graphic form to departmental and agency intelligence consumers. The extent of distribution depends upon the sensitivity of the material involved. Much U.S. intelligence bears the admonition "NOFODIS," for "no foreign distribution."

DOCTOR

KGB term for the police. If an agent suffers an "illness" (i.e., he is arrested), he goes to the "hospital" (jail).

DOORKNOCKER

An agent assigned to do personnel security interviews, to ascertain whether persons needing a security clearance have no nefarious activities in their past. The process begins when the person in question completes a background information form listing such essentials as date and place of birth, parents, educational background, employment history, and (this is where things get tricky) professional and personal references.

Each of these items must be verified by an investigator either from the military intelligence services (if the subject is under arms), the Civil Service Commission (if the subject desires to be a bureaucrat), or the FBI (if the subject wishes to work for the Bureau or in an industrial installation that requires security clearances for employees).

A doorknocker is the footsoldier of the security system and behaves and is treated as such. He often has no information other than the bare notation that the subject lived at such-and-such address for two months, fifteen years earlier, when his father worked for a pipeline company. The impulse is to jot "NV"—"not verifiable"—on the form and go have a beer, but superior powers sprinkle the day's work load with "setups"— tests to insure that the doorknocker is doing what he should.

Doorknockers must endure such other indignities as amorous housewives (who are happy to have a stranger come around unannounced at mid-morning), dogs that bite, people who hate the government and anyone associated with it, and old ladies with cookies and milk and boundless conversation. Whatever the indignity, the doorknocker must elicit a yes or no answer to the key question: "Do you recommend [name of subject] for a position of trust and responsibility with the United States government?"

DOUBLE AGENT

A person who goes to work for one secret service and then changes his allegiance to a rival; he purports to serve both his conflicting masters. Given enough money, he might do just that. The double agent is sometimes confused with the "mole" or "penetration agent," a person whose loyalty lies with the rival power but who joins another cause for duty purposes.

Intelligence archives includes a self-definition of "double agent" by a person who served as such: Colonel Stig Wennerstrom of the Swedish air force, who over a twenty-year period worked for Nazi Germany, the USSR, and the United States. In Wennerstrom's confession, he described a double agent's function: "The one side has an agent whom it deliberately tries to work in as an agent on the other side, of course without the other side knowing anything about it." And, Wennerstrom added, this is "the most advanced and dangerous kind of work an agent can do, both for the agent himself and for the two parties."

DOUBLED

A doubled agent is said to "work under control," or "in harness." He will "play back" bogus messages to his home controller—using texts provided by his captors.

DRY CLEANING

Various techniques a surveillance subject uses to shake off his pursuers or to establish whether he is being followed. Walking a haphazard route, with many turns and changes of course; darting in and out of elevators, department stores, and subway cars; scurrying through obscure exits of churches or cafés—the methods of dry cleaning are as varied as a skilled agent's imagination can contrive.

(During a foot surveillance exercise in downtown Baltimore in the 1950s, the author followed a well-dressed subject who went into a jewelry store and spent almost an hour pricing expensive watches. I attracted so much adverse attention as an obviously impecunious youth in his early twenties, clad in a sports suit and chinos, that the salesmen made signs they were ready to call the cops. When the subject finally left the store, he looked at me—now lurking behind a newspaper across the street—and gave a broad wink. I was not amused.)

DUBOK

Literally, a "little oak" in Russian; in KGB usage, a hiding place for messages. The KGB equivalent of a dead letter drop. The possibilities are limitless.

According to Igor Gouzenko, a Soviet cipher clerk who defected to the Canadians in 1946, the GRU and KGB are particular about the use of *duboks*. As Gouzenko told the Royal Canadian Mounted Police, "The favorite places for a *dubok* are telephone booths (behind the phone box); toilets (inside the water tank); some abandoned stone structure with plenty of splits between the stones—old fences, graveyards, etc. In most cases all places are selected in such a way that access to them is easy but not conspicuous. . . . Sometimes they [Soviet case officers] may use a trick such as this: The contact man sits down on a bench in a casual and relaxed pose. Unnoticed, he may pin a letter under the bench with thumb tacks, then, minutes later, leave the place. Agents may come half an hour later and pick it up. So those who are watching the agent's every movement— even the most unsuspicious and relaxed movements—should check them right away."

KGB people also refer to a letter-drop as a *taynik*.

DUD

A person who makes contact with an intelligence agency with the declared intention of passing information, but who never appears again. (*Blindgaenger*, to the West German intelligence services.)

DYNAMO SPORTS CLUB

KGB's "team" in track and field and other sporting events in the Soviet Union.

e

EARS ONLY

Information so sensitive it is not committed to paper. CIA occasionally briefs Congressional committees on this basis to guard against leaks, witting or otherwise, that could harm an ongoing operation. Ears Only is not a formal classification.

EDIBLE PAPER

Paper, used for writing messages, that is water soluble and that can be swallowed by an intelligence agent during an emergency. The dissolution is slow, and at one stage the paper assumes "the consistency of the plastic dentists use to fit false teeth," in the words of CIA veteran William Hood.

ELICITATION

Obtaining information from an individual or a group in a manner that conceals the true intent of the conversation. For instance, after I returned from a reportorial trip to Cuba in 1964, a Treasury Department intelligence agent asked for the loan of the prints of any photographs I had taken. He expressed curiosity "about general conditions there." Grease pencil markings on the photos when they were returned tipped his true interest: the manufacturer of late-model buses and trucks that had been shipped into Cuba in contravention of the U.S. ban on exports to the Communist island. An agent will often conduct an hour-long interview for the sole purpose of asking a single question to which he needs an answer: "By the way, when the tour bus took you out to Veradero Beach, did you follow the coastal road, or did it go inland for a ways?" The agent does not say flatly, "We understand the Soviets helped the Cubans install surface-to-air missiles outside Havana." The casual American tourist would know only whether the suspected area is now off-limits.

ELINT

Acronym for "electronic intelligence," or the interception of electronic signals from radar, missiles, and the like.

ELSUR INDEX (Electronic Surveillance)

An FBI index containing the names of all persons overheard, even incidentally, on both court-ordered and warrantless electronic surveillances. The ELSUR Index also includes information on the initial date of the monitoring and the name of the target of the surveillance.

ENCIPHER

To convert a plain text message into unintelligible form by the use of a cypher system.

ENCRYPT

To convert a plain text message into unintelligible form by means of a cryptosystem; this term also covers the meaning of "encipher" and "encode."

ESPIONAGE

"Intelligence activity directed toward the acquisition of information through clandestine means and proscribed by the laws of the country against which it is committed," per the Intelligence Community Staff Glossary, June 1978. From the leftist point, "espionage charges against foreign nationals are, like espionage itself, dirty politics by another name," per lawyer Leonard Boudin, who has represented numerous Soviet bloc spies over the years.

ESSENTIAL ELEMENTS OF INFORMATION (EEIs)

A military intelligence term for the most urgently required intelligence data. Depending upon the level of command, EEIs can be momentous or mundane. A theater air commander wishes to know what antiaircraft fire can be expected over a target area. A platoon commander will ask whether a given field is cleared of snipers. The term itself is often forgotten in the hurry of battle; a commander, however, makes known what he desires now and what can wait for tomorrow.

ESTABLISHED SOURCE

The FBI term for a person who has been previously used as an informant by the Bureau. Use of this designation implies that the established source is reliable.

ESTABLISHING BONA FIDES

The use of recognition signals that enables agents unknown to one another to meet and establish contact. *(See also* RECOGNITION SIGNALS.) The usual device is the ostentatious display of a certain newspaper or magazine. A CIA legend features an officer who owned a beagle hound that he loved to use instead of a periodical to establish his bona fides. He cabled another station that he would be arriving, and that the greeter should look for the hound. "LOOK FORWARD TO MEETING YOUR BONO FIDO," came the reply.

EXECUTIVE ACTION

An euphemism for assassination. The term was used in some CIA documents obtained by the Church Committee to describe a program aimed at overthrowing certain foreign leaders, by assassination if necessary. No executive action assassination ever occurred, as the committee stated in its final report to the Senate. The British intelligence services, through MI5 director Sir Dick White, forbade assassination as an instrument of clandestine policy in 1956. A similar order to American intelligence was issued after disclosures that, at Presidential directive, CIA had tried to kill Cuba's Fidel Castro and had been involved in plots against Patrice Lumumba of the Congo.

EXFILTRATION

Smuggling an agent out of an unfriendly country.

EXPENSES

Opening gambit to entrap an intelligence target into working for an intelligence agency. Typically, the recruiting agent asks for an unclassified directory or public document, then insists on paying the person "for your trouble." After several such "favors," the agent asks that the person "sign a receipt for my records, so that I can be reimbursed for expenses." Once the person signs, he is hooked.

EXPLOITATION

The process of obtaining information from any source and taking full advantage of it for strategic or tactical purposes. Exploitation can be public and direct. For instance, when CIA obtained the text of Soviet Premier Khrushchev's scathing attack on Josef Stalin at a party conference in 1956, there was brisk internal debate over what use to make of the information. The decision was to give the document to *The New York Times,* which (as anticipated) published the full text. The impact upon world Communism was staggering; CIA's hand was not publicly revealed, although generally suspected. A cruder attempt at exploitation was the FBI's sub rosa circulation of tape recordings of the Rev. Martin Luther King, Jr., at sexual play. The damage to King's image as a civil rights leader was transitory; the grubbiness of the operation tarnished the reputation of FBI director J. Edgar Hoover even after his death.

EXTERMINATORS
See BUG.

EXTERNAL COLLECTION PROGRAM

Periodic visits by security officers of the National Security Agency to bars, restaurants, and other establishments in the area around NSA headquarters at Fort Meade, Maryland. The visits were made to determine whether NSA employees, in their after-hours gathering, discussed classified information, and whether "agents of hostile intelligence services frequented these locations," according to the Church Committee's final report. The "program" also involved alerting bartenders and other employees to report suspicious conversations. This bar-hopping lasted from 1963 until 1967, when NSA security men decided they "lacked the personnel to carry on such a program."

EYE CLUB, I CLUB

An informal liaison group, social in nature, of British intelligence officers who work for the established intelligence service, the military, and the Foreign Office.

f

FALSE CONFIRMATION

A delicate phase of a disinformation or deception operation intended to give credence to the item of information being passed to the other side. Typically, the false confirmation would come from a source not readily identifiable with the persons or agencies involved in the major phase of the operation.

An example: The CIA station in London receives a high-level KGB defector and decides he can be put to more efficient use if the USSR believes him to be dead. An ambulance makes a conspicuous sirens-blaring visit to a known CIA safe house and drives away with a person on a stretcher. Attendants at the hospital to which the defector is taken are led to believe that he arrived dead, victim of poisoning. A "body" is removed in a sealed casket. Shortly thereafter, the head of the station's counterintelligence section is relieved of duty and returned to assignment in the United States, and rumors are set afloat that he was disgraced because of his "mishandling" of the defector, who killed himself while in custody.

Now the kicker: An advisory memorandum is circulated to other Western intelligence agencies alerting them of a new method KGB agents have of concealing poison capsules on their persons, one unknown even to their superiors. The memorandum disclaims any knowledge of how widespread such use might be, but notes that KGB officials keep it secret even from their superiors so that they have the option of committing suicide if they fall into disfavor. The memorandum also states that a KGB person might use the capsule if he has a change of heart during the midst of a defection. Once this memorandum is learned of by the KGB it confirms more effectively than any previous information the death of the defector that CIA has alive.

Credibility, of course, is the key factor. The operative rule is

to let the "false confirmation" come to light through efforts of
the other side, so that it is not a patent plant.

FALSE FLAG

Recruiting an agent or an informer through the guise of tell-
ing him the actual work will be done for another country or
interest. False flagging is used when the potential recruit would
not likely accept a direct approach from the country desiring his
services. Harry Rositzke, long a Soviet specialist for CIA, cites
an example: "In 1950 two American Jewish counterintelligence
officers were recruited in Vienna by a Soviet intelligence officer
masquerading as an Israeli." The FBI has encountered several
instances in which KGB agents managed to pass themselves off
as highly conservative Americans when recruiting right-wing
government employees as informants. The pitch was that they
should report on the workings of their agency "to help my
patriotic organization to be sure the Commies aren't infiltrating
our institutions." As former CIA officer David Atlee Phillips
has written, "Today there are unsuspecting zealots around the
world who are managed and paid as spies; they sell their countries' secrets believing all the while they are helping 'the good
guys.' "

FAMILY JEWELS

The self-admitted list of transgressions of the CIA charter
compiled by its officials in 1973, following revelations that
Watergate figures E. Howard Hunt and G. Gordon Liddy had
used Agency facilities in some of their illegal activities. James
Schlesinger, the then-DCI, on May 9, 1973, ordered "all the
senior operating officials of this Agency to report to me immediately on any activities now going on, or that have gone on in
the past, which might be construed to be outside the legislative
charter of this Agency." Working the resultant reports, CIA's
Office of the Inspector General compiled 693 pages of "potential flap activities," including the bugging of newsmen in hopes
of tracing leaks of classified materials, Operation CHAOS
against the anti-war movement, experiments with mind control
drugs, and a mail-intercept program—some 300 items in all. To
the lasting dismay of many Agency veterans, Schlesinger's successor, William Colby, a few months later yielded to political

and public pressure and surrendered the list to the Rockefeller Commission, the first of several bodies to probe CIA over the next few years. By handing over the family jewels—a euphemism for testicles—Colby was said to have helped in the emasculation of the Agency that he had served for decades.

FARM, THE
See CAMP PEARY.

FEEDBACK AGENT
A hostile agent planted within a rival intelligence organization who informs his superiors of the success or lack thereof of its own counterespionage operations. Also known as a "penetration agent," for having penetrated a rival service.

FERRET SEARCHES
Surprise "inspections" by agents of CIA's Office of Security. These officers are authorized to search even the personal homes or apartments of station chiefs to insure that no security procedures are being violated (such as bringing classified material home for use in a nonsecure area). Ferret searches are also used when an agency employee is suspected of illicit activity. Many are done with such discretion that the target does not realize that his lodgings have been "tossed" (searched). The privacy invasion means that ferret searches and the men who conduct them are not loved by their colleagues.

FIELD INFORMATION REPORTS (FIRs)
The basic reporting form of a CIA operative or contract employee working in the field. These are submitted directly to the CIA station, initialed by the station chief or his deputy, and sent by diplomatic pouch to Langley. Urgent FIRs are upgraded and sent by secure wireless.

FIFTH COLUMN
Term denoting subversives willing to work for the enemy within their own country. Although given wide popular use during World War II, "fifth column" is now considered archaic; the modern CIA and FBI version is "agents of influence."

In his play *The Fifth Column,* Ernest Hemingway wrote, "Oh, they always shoot from the windows at night during the bombardment. The fifth column people. The people who fight us from inside the city."

Attorney General Robert Jackson in 1940 defined the fifth column as "that portion of our population which is ready to give assistance or encouragement in any form to invading or opposing ideologies."

President Roosevelt recognized the danger of a fifth column in America in a memorandum, dated May 21, 1940, to Attorney General Francis Biddle authorizing wiretapping in "grave matters involving the defense of the nation." As Roosevelt wrote, "It is . . . well known that certain other nations have been engaged in the organization of propaganda of so-called 'fifth-column' in other countries and in preparation for sabotage, as well as in actual sabotage. It is too late to do anything about it after sabotage, assassinations and 'fifth column' activities are completed."

FIREFLY

A chemical that spontaneously ignites—after a bit—when mixed with gasoline. OSS developed Firefly and used it to great effect during World War II on German trucks and tanks. Latter-day variants of Firefly are still to be found in CIA and other arsenals of unconventional weaponry. Although the compound is simple, its exact composition is best left undescribed.

FIX

A CIA term, of Cold War origin, that refers to a person who is to be compromised or blackmailed so that he will do the Agency's bidding. As intelligence historian Donald McCormick notes, "Those seeking out the possibilities of employing such tactics talk of a 'low-key' fix or an OK fix; the latter is actual blackmail."

FLAP POTENTIAL

The risk of embarrassment to an intelligence agency stemming from disclosure of an illegal or questionable activity, or of the defection of an agent. The agency's first impulse is concealment of the mishap (the British, for instance, delayed for days before confirming the 1951 defection of the spies Maclean and

Burgess). Former CIA official Miles Copeland states that the "frantic inquiries intelligence agencies used to make when leaks were suspected are now a thing of the past." By Copeland's testimony, the mode now is the "quiet flap," in which investigations are conducted with extreme discretion, so as not to alert other persons involved that they are suspect. The quiet approach also means that persons caught red-handed are often permitted to go free (although in unemployed fashion) rather than make a public appearance in court to answer criminal charges.

Another type of flap potential situation concerned numerous illegal CIA and FBI surveillance and mail-opening operations of the 1950s and 1960s. The FBI under Director J. Edgar Hoover had a direct rule of thumb in handling flaps, potential or otherwise: "Don't embarrass the Bureau." But CIA's James J. Angleton, the counterintelligence chief, suggested that CIA develop a cover story for the mail intercepts to the effect that the project involved "certain research work on foreign mail . . ." Another Agency official stated that, if there should be an accidental compromise, the "Office of Security would utilize its official cover to explain any difficulties . . ." This official noted that "high level police contacts with the New York Police Department are enjoyed, which would preclude any uncontrolled inquiry in the event police action was indicated." If any citizens griped about lost mail, they should be referred to the Post Office. And if a disgruntled CIA employee revealed the intercept program, the charge would "be answered by complete denial of the activity."

FLAPS AND SEALS

A mail-opening course taught by the CIA's Technical Services Division beginning in the early 1950s as part of HT-LINGUAL. The basic method was simple. Glue on envelopes was softened by steam from a kettle. Carefully wielding a narrow stick, the agent pried open the envelope and took out the letter. One agent who took the flaps and seals course told the Church Committee that "you could do it with your own teapot at home." Skilled interceptors could open an envelope in five to fifteen seconds.

Ever conscious of technology, Technical Services Division in the 1960s developed a sort of "steam oven" designed to open one hundred letters simultaneously. But the dissolved glue often hardened before letters could be extricated; there was also an occasional mix-up of letters and envelopes, so that a citizen in Murmansk received a message intended for someone else's aunt in Kiev. So the HT-LINGUAL agents returned to their trusted kettle-and-stick method.

The FBI, not to be outdone by its intelligence rival, later developed an opening process said to require only a second or two for a single letter (contrasted with the five to fitfteen seconds for CIA). But one CIA man familiar with the FBI method termed it "sloppy . . . they'd have ink running all over the page." *(See also* CHAMFERING.)

FLASH-ALIAS DOCUMENTS
See BACKSTOPPING.

FLOATER
A person used for a one-time or occasional intelligence job; low-level and, often as not, unwitting. For instance, MI5 might recruit a Charing Cross call girl to accompany a foreign diplomat on his evening rounds, simply to ascertain where he goes and to whom he talks.

FLOATING CONTACT
A surveillance subject who suddenly gets into a passing car or taxi. When this occurs, the surveillance team goes into an "all-skate"—the deployment of as many cars as are available to keep up the chase.

FLUTTER
The polygraph test administered to information-sensitive officers of the American intelligence community, both at the time of their recruitment and then on or close to the annual anniversary of their employment. Subjects are asked such questions as whether they have stolen money, engaged in homosexual or other offbeat sexual conduct, committed adultery, or compromised secrets. Although the accuracy of a polygraph is widely debated, its use is a key tool of the security offices of CIA, NSA, DIA, and other intelligence agencies.

FORCED INTERROGATION
KGB questioning in which the severity of the subject's treatment is decided by the men wielding the truncheons; essentially, they can do anything they wish, physically or psychologically, to achieve the desired results. The subject, between sessions, is kept in a lighted, windowless cell; the interrogations are scheduled in no discernible time pattern, so that he quickly loses any concept of time. Food (and not very much of it) is also served at random times. Once the prisoner is disoriented and realizes he has no chance of freedom, he generally does what the interrogators wish. The Soviets honed these techniques in preparing for Stalin's purge trials of the 1930s; they are now augmented by the use of drugs.

FORCING
Making such harsh demands on an agent—such as demanding that he obtain information beyond his capabilities—that he disrupts his normal regimen and attracts attention to himself. "Forcing" is a grave violation of trade-craft, for it jeopardizes human life.

FORCING THE TONGUE
The skilled interrogator's trick of persuading the subject to speak in his native tongue, which gives him the misguided confidence that he is "with his own kind." Doing an interrogation in a foreign language, conversely, reminds the subject to keep up his defenses.

FORT HOLABIRD
The long-time site of the Army Intelligence School, on the eastern outskirts of Baltimore. "The Bird" was also headquarters of the Army Intelligence Command during the frostier days of the Cold War. Originally an Army locomotive repair depot, Holabird was the training ground for a generation of CIC and Field Operations Intelligence (FOI) operatives. Many of the latter, in the 1950s, were Eastern Europeans of fierce anti-Communist bent who spoke scant English and who were allowed off the Bird only under controlled circumstances. They did considerable damage to saloons along Dundalk Avenue. They then went away to Eastern Europe on covert missions. CIC trainees

undertook either the "A Course," for analysts, or the "B Course," for field agents. Mostly recent college graduates, they had the good sense to keep away from the FOI areas. Holabird also housed the Central Records Facility, the repository for every intelligence report ever received by the United States Army. Persons assigned there slaved as file clerks, their tedium broken by the fact that they had ready access to a section entitled "Perversions, Sexual—US ARMY Ex-CONUS," which featured depositions by and photographs of persons caught in awfully awkward circumstances.

Fort Huachuca, Arizona, is now the headquarters of U.S. Army intelligence and most of the activities formerly pursued at Fort Holabird. The training ground of uncountable hundreds of military spooks is now an industrial park being developed by the city of Baltimore. The only government functions surviving is a Justice Department safe house for important (and vulnerable) witnesses in criminal trials. The safe house was once the main classroom building of the Army Intelligence School.

FRENCH ROOM

The conference room of the director of Central Intelligence, so named for reasons no one remembers.

FRIEND

A person persuaded to influence a foreign government, or some segment thereof. His motives are almost unfailingly ideological (a term that extends to protecting the family fortune). Such a Friend is numbered among a CIA station's most valued assets, because his initial commitment means that he will be willing to perform late-hour odd jobs as well. (For instance, if a CIA officer in Rome needs a car and guide to drive to an obscure town at 2:00 A.M., the Friend is apt to oblige.)

FRIENDS

Operatives of British MI6, or foreign intelligence service. During World War II, being a Friend was highly secret—so much so that when Heinrich Himmler of the Nazi SS gave a public speech disclosing the names of all the most important Friends, from their chief downward, the translated text was promptly classified "Most Secret." Fitzroy Maclean, himself a

Friend before entering Parliament, noted that his socially aware colleagues composed their reports on "sheets of deep blue writing paper of the kind then affected by many society hostesses."

FSR (Foreign Service Reserve)

The rank the State Department insisted be given to CIA officials working abroad under diplomatic cover through the late 1960s. State refused to permit CIA people to be integrated into their family as Foreign Service Officers (or FSOs). Since the FSR designation was printed in the State Department *Biographical Register* and embassy directories, little imagination was required for outsiders to spot CIA officers. Such anti-CIA publications as *Counterspy* used the FSR label to identify hundreds of supposedly covert CIA operatives working under embassy cover during the early 1970s.

FUMIGATE

To use electronic counter-devices to locate and neutralize listening devices concealed in a room. Horst Schwirkmann, of the West German intelligence service—one of the best fumigators in the business in the 1950s and 1960s—paid dearly for a prank he played on the KGB in Moscow. During a routine fumigation, Schwirkmann playfully rigged a device that emitted a high-frequency sound in the bugs he had just discovered. The sound not only severely damaged the KGB's receivers but also caused much pain to technicians listening in at the time. Several days later a KGB man surreptitiously doused Schwirkmann's leg with mustard gas as he walked in a Moscow park. For two days Schwirkmann lingered on the brink of death. He survived but was disabled for weeks.

FUNKSPIEL

German for "radio game," which in World War II was the German equivalent of the British "Operation Double-Cross." During the war more than half the clandestine radio stations in occupied Europe—Soviet, British and others—came under control of German military counterintelligence or the Gestapo. In uncountable instances the Germans "persuaded" arrested foreign spies to continue transmissions to their headquarters, using messages composed by German intelligence. Agents dispatched from England parachuted to certain detention, and death. To the Abwehr, the change of loyalty by Allied agents was called *umdrehen,* or "turning around." *(See also* OPERATION DOUBLE-CROSS.)

The most famed funkspiel operation mounted by the Germans was NORDPOL, with both the Dutch and the British as victims. For some eighteen months, arrested Dutch agents continued communications with bases in England; at one time, fourteen "Dutch" radio stations actually worked for the Germans. NORDPOL resulted in the arrests of more than sixty British and Dutch agents who parachuted onto the continent.

FUSAG

Abbreviation for First United States Army Group, the totally fictional "force" created by Allied intelligence in 1943–44 and passed off to the Axis as the intended invasion army. FUSAG was part of the elaborate panoply of disinformation operations intended to shield the exact time, place, and composition of the invasion.

g

GAS-GUN

A KGB assassination device capable of firing a burst of poison into the face of the intended victim. One version widely used in Western Europe in the 1950s consisted of a tube some seven inches long and slightly larger than a man's finger, with a firing pin and trigger at one end. The tube consisted of three sections. The trigger, when pulled, caused the firing pin to ignite a powder charge in the center section, which in turn crushed a glass phial in the third. The glass phial contained five cc. of hydrocyanide, which would vaporize upon contact with the air. According to the European intelligence expert Louis Edmund Hagen, "Held about two feet from a person's face, it would kill instantly, no trace being left on the victim. By swallowing a pill containing an antidote (amyl nitrate) beforehand, and by inhaling the vapour of another antidote released by crushing a glass phial immediately after the weapon had been fired, the operator of the gun could avoid being affected by his own poison."

Two persons killed by this sinister device were anti-Communist Ukrainian Nationalists in West Germany—Lev Rebet, editor of an exile newspaper in Munich, considered a prime enemy of the USSR and the KGB, and Stephan Bandera, head of the Organization of the Ukrainian Nationalist Revolution, or OUNR. Both were murdered by Bogdan Stashinsky, a Ukrainian forced into KGB service after committing a petty crime while a university student. As a reward for these murders, committed in 1957 and 1959, Stashinsky received the Order of the Red Banner from Andrew Shelepin, director of the KGB. Conscience eventually overcame Stashinsky; he defected and, after persuasion, convinced West German security authorities of his role in the killings. He was sent to prison for eight years, the judge stating, "The sentence pronounced by this court is not intended to destroy the accused. It is to help him atone."

GAMMA SHEETS

One-time code pads used by Soviet agencies; printed on flash paper that vanishes if touched with a match.

GEHLEN ORGANIZATION

The German intelligence apparatus, seized intact by the American CIC in 1945 and put to work for the West. Its commander, General Reinhard Gehlen, ran Hitler's military espionage in Russia during World War II. Captured, Gehlen turned over his mammoth files and network of spies to the United States, and he ultimately became chief of the West German intelligence agency, the *BnD,* working directly under CIA. Pragmatism outweighed revulsion in the instance of Gehlen, and he gave Western agencies invaluable aid in the immediate postwar years.

Hectored by a leftist Congressman about the Gehlen connection, President Truman retorted, "Well, we've also worked with another Hitler collaborator, a man *you* admire." Who? The congressman queried. "Joe Stalin," Truman replied. "Remember, he signed on with Hitler in 1939. This Gehlen fellow, I don't care if he fucks goats. If he helps us, we'll use him."

GETTING ONE FOOT INTO THE ORGANIZATION

The first toehold a prospective double agent gains in a rival intelligence agency. Most frequently, the double agent agrees to sell inconsequential information for money, which at once establishes his bona fides and which "obligates" him to the agency making the payment. A common opening ploy for Army Counterintelligence Corps agents in West Germany in the 1950s was to offer Communist agents a phone book for the U.S. headquarters command in Stuttgart, classified "For Official Use Only." The information contained therein was worthless, but the transactions permitted CIC to pass off numerous persons as "doubles."

GHETTO INFORMANT PROGRAM

A special FBI program to elicit intelligence on the black community, especially in urban areas, during 1967–73. Attorney General Ramsey Clark initiated the program in a letter to FBI Director J. Edgar Hoover in September 1967, citing a "widespread belief that there is more organized activity in the riots than we presently know about . . . [W]e must make certain that every attempt is being made to get all information bearing upon these problems . . . and . . . to determine the identity of the people and interests involved . . ." The FBI, in implementing Ramsey Clark's order, defined a ghetto informant as "an individual who lives and works in a ghetto area and has access to information regarding the racial situation and racial activities in the area which he furnished to the Bureau on a confidential basis." As examples, the FBI cited "the proprietor of a candy store and barbershop" in an urban ghetto area. The first GIs were passive listening posts; later, the Bureau encouraged them to undertake specific assignments, such as to survey bookstores specializing in black publications to determine "if militant extremist literature is available therein."

GO-AWAY

A signal given by an agent that it would be unwise to make a prearranged contact in a public place. A go-away is included in the basic instructions to the agent and the person with whom he should make contact. The go-away can take many forms. In the passive sense, the party suspecting surveillance lets his hands dangle free as he walks past his contact. In the active sense, the party thrusts his hands into his pockets. (The variations are as many as a human's imagination.) Active-passive signals shift on odd-even days of the month, thus requiring alertness by both parties.

GO PRIVATE

To break away from the intelligence community, usually with stolen funds, and to attempt to establish a new life elsewhere under a different identity. CIA has an elaborate job-placement service for employees who wish to work elsewhere. So, too, do the British services. But the KGB and its affiliated organizations tend to send "retirees" to Siberia, or worse. Hence the word that a KGB official has decided to go private sends pulses of excitement through the relevant CIA station.

GO TO GROUND

To disappear, to go into hiding. An agent who suspects he is under surveillance, or other suspicion, seemingly drops off the face of the earth. Having a suspect go to ground, and not being able to retrieve him readily, can put a counterespionage agent's career in severe jeopardy. If the suspect reappears, he is said to have "surfaced."

GRADUATED

A Soviet mole who succeeds in moving from one job to a more sensitive position—for instance, from an American newspaper position into the State Department.

GRANNY

A non-Agency employee. (See OBSERVATION POSTS.)

GRAYMAIL

The threat by a defendant in an intelligence-related prosecution to disclose classified information in open court. His intent is to dissuade the government from pressing criminal charges. Several times in the early 1970s, graymail threats caused the United States government to abandon prosecutions of persons with intelligence backgrounds. In response, Congress passed the "graymail act"—formally, the Classified Information Procedures Act—which spells out pretrial procedures that a defendant must follow if he intends to attempt to use classified material in the trial. The trial judge first must review the evidence in secret and decide whether it is in fact germane to the case. The first defendant to invoke the graymail procedures under the act was the rogue American intelligence officer Edwin P. Wilson, who hired himself out as a terrorist trainer for the nefarious dictator Muamar Quaddafi of Libya. Five separate federal judges listened to Wilson's "evidence" that he actually worked for U.S. intelligence while in Libya, and each rejected him. Wilson now serves a multi-decade federal prison term.

Graymail is an old and recurring problem. In the 1950s, an officer in the CIA station in Rome was found to be padding receipts he obtained from his informants and pocketing the extra money. Confronted, he fled all the way to Mexico before being induced to surrender. But as William Colby, then in the Rome station, lamented, "CIA and the Justice Department concluded that he could not be prosecuted without exposing his entire operation and the Italian recipients, and destroying them among their associates." The agent resigned in disgrace but was not punished in court.

GRAY MAN, THE

The intelligence community's term for the perfect operator, "so inconspicuous that he can never catch the waiter's eye in a restaurant," in the words of former director of Central Intelligence William Colby. Short, frail, and bespectacled, Colby felt that his "deliberate cultivation" of the gray man image helped make him a successful spy during his years in the field.

GRAY PROPAGANDA

Statements or publications where the source is nonattributed or deliberately confusing. For some two decades Radio Free Europe (RFE) purported to be an independent, privately financed broadcast apparatus directed against the Soviet bloc. RFE even ran public service ads (i.e., donated by the publication) in major American periodicals asking for donations to continue its crusade. In fact, the bulk of RFE's money—and the sum of its policy direction—came from CIA. The cover was thin and fooled few discerning persons, either American or Soviet. In 1961, I heard a high RFE official plead for contributions from a group of Philadelphia business executives at a Union League luncheon. A tycoon arose and asked, "Why can't the United States government support your program? God knows but we pay enough taxes." The RFE official replied, "The government contribution is substantial, but we want your participation anyway." I was at the luncheon as a reporter, and I knew from some earlier experiences the source of the "government contributions" the RFE official mentioned. For mischief, I approached him after the luncheon and asked, "What percent of your budget does CIA meet now, eighty or ninety?" He flushed, stammered, demanded my name and organization, and within the hour had telephoned at least three news executives at my paper. As I told an inquiring RFE—read, CIA—security officer later, my sole purpose was to impress upon this turkey the fact that covert operations are more easily kept private if one does not gabble about them before luncheon groups with news reporters present. The security officer agreed.

GRINDER

A debriefing room used to interrogate defectors. CIA maintains numerous such facilities within one hundred miles of the Washington area. Soviet defectors who have "gone through the grinder" report they were housed and fed in an adjacent room and given no idea as to their whereabouts (CIA prefers to keep such locales secret from KGB to avoid attempts to kill defectors). The grinding process requires the subject to repeat his story over and over again, in minute detail, while tape recorders run. What he says is double-checked against verifiable information. As many as six months can be required to prove a defector's bona fides. The strain is mental rather than physical, but no KGB defector has anything nice to say about his stay in the grinder.

GRU (Glavnoe Razvedyvatelnoe Upravlenie)

The chief intelligence directorate of the Soviet General Staff —i.e., the Soviet military intelligence group. For foreign intelligence, GRU far surpasses KGB, both in money and manpower —and quite probably in accomplishments. Its alumni include Richard Sorge, who spied in Tokyo under cover as a pro-Nazi German journalist just before World War II, and the atomic spies who hastened along Soviet nuclear development.

GRU is headquartered in an anonymous two-story stone building near the old Khodinsk field at Moscow's Central Airport. Perhaps appropriately, all windows face inward toward a courtyard. No one, not even a ranking official, is permitted to carry a briefcase into the building, and leashed ferocious watchdogs roam the premises. GRU is identified only as "Military Department 44388"; the letters GRU (and their meaning) are unknown to the ordinary Soviet. GRU's main spy school on Militia Street in Moscow, a pleasant building with Georgian columns and an iron lattice fence is simply "Military Department 35576."

GRU's foreign spying is done primarily through its military attachés abroad, supplemented by the industrial espionage operations of its Military-Industrial Commission, or VPK by its Russian initials. The VPK's annual "requirements book" is said to number at least six hundred pages, chiefly running to electronics and space equipment sought in the West. Its budget for such acquisitions is said to be bottomless.

GRU and KGB are unfriendly rivals; they work in tandem only under duress. GRU maintains its own communications system from foreign embassies to Moscow, and GRU agents have their own *rezident* (although in smaller embassies economy dictates closer cooperation). Such Soviet enterprises as Aeroflot, the USSR airline, provide cover. At one time in the late 1970s, nine of eleven Aeroflot employees in the United States were GRU operatives, according to FBI sources.

GRU runs its own assassination squads abroad. Neither service can kill the other's agents—with sanction.

GUERRILLAS

"An organized band of individuals in enemy-held territory, indefinite as to number, which conducts against the enemy irregular operations, including those of a military or quasi-military nature."—OSS definition. *(See also* RESISTANCE GROUP.)

GUIDANCE

"The general direction of an intelligence effort, particularly in the area of collection," according to the Church Committee.

h

HANDLING AGENT

The FBI agent responsible for directing the undercover activities of an informant. According to the FBI Manual, the handling agent "should not only collect information, but direct the informant, be aware of his activities, and maintain such a close relationship that he knows informant's attitude towards the Bureau." The handling agent is also responsible for having the informant submit a written report, or else sign transcriptions of his oral reports. A limited exception to this rule exists for extremist informants who may submit oral reports in cases of imminent violence.

HARD TARGETS

The closed and secret societies of the Soviet Union, the People's Republic of China, and their satellites, as contrasted to the "soft" targets of neutral and allied nations. Hard targeting became the primary emphasis of CIA intelligence gathering in the early 1970s, for several reasons. Too much money was being spent on useless information (such as internal struggles in the French Communist Party). Agents in the field tended to concentrate on easy-to-obtain information, rather than going "into the guts of the enemy." Hard targeting was a prime accomplishment of Richard Helms, the then-DCI.

HARMONICA BUG

A minute transistorized transmitter that can be placed inside the mouthpiece of a telephone handset. One version is in a permanent listening mode so that any conversations in the room can be monitored and transmitted to a listening post nearby. Another (the most commonly used) is activated only when the phone is being employed for a conversation. Mossad has yet another version that contains a small charge of *plastique* explosive. After the subject has been exploited to Mossad's satisfaction, an electronic impulse makes the harmonica bug explode, to the fatal discomfort of whomever happens to be using the telephone at the time.

HEAD OFFICE

The headquarters, in Pullach, West Germany, of the Gehlen Organization, that nation's long-time supreme intelligence organization. Pullach was officially secret for years, although well known to the KGB through the evil offices of double agent Heinze Felfe, who worked a decade for both Gehlen and KGB. Felfe's photographs and physical descriptions gave KGB perhaps a more intimate knowledge of Pullach than that of the building engineer.

HEAVY MOB, HEAVY SQUAD

Officers of girth and muscle the CIA uses in situations where brute strength is more important than finesse; i.e., when a defector must be brought through an airport, and the KGB is apt to try a kidnap or a killing. The FBI version is the heavy squad. Men of the heavy mob also do bodyguard duty for the DCI and other top Agency officers.

HEDDY

A simulated aerial bomb that duplicates the noise of a falling bomb, intended to create confusion and fear in the target city. The Heddy, weighing only about two ounces, was an OSS creation for World War II. A delayed fuse activates several seconds after the Heddy is dropped from an airplane. The device produces a whistling sound for 2½ to 3½ seconds, after which the explosive charge detonates, producing a sound similar to that of a large firecracker. OSS used the Heddy to clear areas into which it intended to parachute agents. A secondary use was to harass factory sites to disrupt war production.

HEEL-LIFT

A CIA gadget that causes the wearer to walk with a slight limp—a thick leather pad that is inserted into one shoe. A wadded-up handkerchief will suffice in an emergency. The changed gait, along with other disguise techniques, is intended to change the wearer's appearance.

HOLIDAY ESPIONAGE

Odd-job missions performed by intelligence agents during the course of casual trips away from their home station. The "vacation"—often legitimate—provides the cover story for the travel. For instance, Colonel Stig Wennerstrom, the Swedish traitor, spied for the Soviets while on vacation trips to Wiesbaden, West Germany, and Spain. In the words of Swedish journalist H. K. Ronblom, who wrote the definitive book on the Wennerstrom case, "A few weeks' holiday association with people from whom it was possible to extract a little information was practically risk-free." One specific mission performed by Wennerstrom during his holiday spying was to ascertain the state of U.S. military alert during the 1958 Lebanon crisis. Wennerstrom visited an American air force officer stationed in West Germany with whom he was friendly and wheedled from him the fact that the United States was alerting paratroopers for possible deployment in Lebanon.

In reality, no intelligence officer is ever fully on holiday, for the professional is constantly alert for information of intelligence value—even bus and subway schedules and local maps.

HONEY TRAP

Sexual entrapment for intelligence purposes, usually to put a target into a compromising situation so that he or she can be blackmailed. According to the British intelligence expert Robert Moss, the Cuban DGI once gave press credentials to classy Havana hookers and set up a call-girl operation targeted at UN officials. But the operation had to be aborted hastily when the Cubans realized the whores' principal clients were Soviets.

HOSPITAL

KGB euphemism for a prison to which an agent has been sent. *(See also* DOCTOR.)

HT-LINGUAL

Cover name for a CIA mail-intercept project that lasted more than 20 years and involved the opening of some 215,000 letters to and from the Soviet Union that were read and photographed by agents in a special facility in New York. (HT-LINGUAL was the term used by CIA's Counterespionage Staff; the Office of Security, also involved in the operation, used the code-name SR-POINTER).

HT-LINGUAL started with a request by CIA's Soviet Division (SR) in early 1952—supported by other ranking agency officials—that Soviet mail be scanned, and that the names and addresses of correspondents be recorded by hand. The intent was fivefold; according to a CIA memorandum of July 1, 1952:

- Furnish much live ammunition for psychological warfare;
- produce subjects, who if proven loyal to the United States, might be good agent material because of their contacts within the Soviet Union;
- offer documentary material for reproduction and subsequent use by our own agents;
- produce intelligence information when read in the light of other known factors and events; and
- create a channel for sending communications to American agents inside the Soviet Union.

Although the original HT-LINGUAL project involved only the recording of exteriors of envelopes, CIA counterintelligence chief James J. Angleton noted that some mail was opened by agents "swiping a letter, processing it at night, and returning it the next day." At Angleton's behest, Richard Helms, then the director of CIA clandestine services (Operations), approved expanding HT-LINGUAL in 1955 to include systematic opening. Postal officials assigned CIA a "secure" room at LaGuardia Airport where mail could be opened and photographed. Selected letters were also screened for secret writing and microdots; CIA even developed techniques for opening mail sealed with "the more difficult and sophisticated adhesives."

In later assessments, HT-LINGUAL's contribution to intelligence was disputed. Although HT-LINGUAL produced many "operational leads," few of these were converted into actual operations. The SR (Soviet Union) Division of CIA found some occasional items of interest; Clandestine Services, on the other hand, downgraded HT-LINGUAL's value, and the Office of Security found its product to be "of very little value . . . meager . . ."

HT-LINGUAL eventually led to a jurisdictional squabble between CIA and the FBI. In the mid-1950s, the FBI arrested the Soviet master spy Rudolph Abel, and also learned of the existence of three other ranking agents. Yet the bureau was stymied in trying to find the link between these agents and their controls. On January 10, 1958, an allied nation's counterintelligence agency (most likely the Gehlen Organization of West Germany) told the FBI of a specific address in the Soviet Union used as a mail drop for agents abroad. When the FBI tried to institute a watch program for Soviet mail, it stumbled headlong onto HT-LINGUAL. After a brisk bureaucratic tussle, CIA retained control of the intercept program, with the FBI receiving reports on the requested targets. *(See also* MAIL COVER.)

HUFF DUFF

Communications jargon for High Frequency Direction Finding (HF/DF).

HUMINT

Human intelligence; i.e., information derived from a live source, such as an agent-in-place. Basically, good old-fashioned espionage," comments CIC figure Bruce A. Trinque.

i

IDENTIFIERS

Soviet term for an informant who can identify persons of intelligence interest or of suspicious ideology. SMERSH made wide use of identifiers in screening Russian repatriates who, for one reason or another, had been outside the USSR during World War II. Stalin insisted that each of these five to six million expatriates be returned to the USSR, voluntarily or otherwise. The word of the identifier often determined whether they went to the Gulag, to the gallows, or to a civilian life.

ILLEGAL

An intelligence agent who operates in a target country without the benefit of official status. He lives under an assumed or created identity, and has minimal or no contact with his nation's overt representatives.

If CIA has ever succeeded in planting an illegal inside the Soviet Union, no such case has ever been publicized. The Soviets, however, have taken advantage of the open American society to run literally scores of illegals into the United States—the most notable being Rudolph Ivanovich Abel, a colonel in KGB, who lived undetected in New York for eight years. (After arrest he was traded for U-2 pilot Francis Gary Powers.)

Normal overseas tours for KGB illegals are for seven years, the amount of time required to meld into the target nation and be of operational value. Even though the illegal might have a wife and family in the USSR, his only contact is via an occasional microdot letter smuggled to him with his "official" communiques. The illegal is often supplied with a nominal "wife" who is also trained in covert activities and who performs such support functions as radio operator; these pairings also provide both parties with a sexual outlet, thereby enabling them to avoid romantic entanglements that might endanger their missions. A firm KGB rule requires an illegal to be married before he leaves the USSR on his first mission, and a start on a family is vigorously encouraged. The concern of KGB is not familial, however: the spymasters know the existence of a wife and child —as hostages, literally—are a degree of insurance against defection. At least one defector has told Western intelligence that his first "vacation" after seven years in the field was extended for several months until his KGB superiors were satisfied that his wife was pregnant.

ILLNESS
KGB euphemism for an agent who has been arrested. *(See also* DOCTOR.)

INDICATOR ORGANIZATION
A group deemed typical of others working toward a common political or philosophical goal. When assets are limited, an intelligence agency will single out a particular organization for intensive coverage, on the theory that its activities will reflect those of similarly oriented groups. Given the lock-step workings of Communist-dominated front groups in, say, the anti-nuclear movement, close scrutiny of a single organization tells the FBI what it needs to know.

INDISPENSABLES
Former Nazi intelligence and counterintelligence experts taken into the Gehlen Organization of West Germany in the late 1940s and early 1950s. Ironically, much of their work was against the extreme right (the political grouping from which they had come) rather than the Communists. The indispensables also worked for Dr. Otto John, the controversial head of the *BfV (Bundesamt für Verfassungsschutz),* or Federal Office for the Protection of the Constitution, charged with keeping both left and right extremists away from the government and out of key organizations in labor, the press, and private associations. John mysteriously disappeared into East Germany in the 1950s, the announced victim of a kidnapping. Such, too, was the story he told on his return to the West a year later. In fact, John had

worked as a Communist agent for years, and he was carefully isolated from any further significant work in intelligence.

INFILTRATION

The placing of an agent in a target area within hostile territory or within a targeted organization. The FBI effectively used infiltration to gain intelligence on Fascist and Communist groups beginning in the late 1930s. The bureau, at Presidential direction, used the same technique in the 1960s in trying to confirm foreign financing of extreme anti-war groups. The Congressional outcry was so shrill that the practice was abandoned; the stricture extends even to infiltration of avowed terrorist groups.

INFORMANT

A person who wittingly or unwittingly gives information of intelligence value to an agent or the service for which he works. There are two broad types of informants: those an intelligence agency first recruits and then inserts into the target group or country; and those who are already in place and who are "turned" (recruited) as informants. Such persons are the backbone of any intelligence or law enforcement organization; consequently agents spend a considerable portion of time in their recruitment and care.

The FBI further categorizes its informants. "Subversive" informants are those used to investigate "activities aimed at overthrowing, destroying or undermining the Government of the United States or any of its political subdivisions by illegal means." Those in the other category, "extremist" informants, have their mandate extended to include investigation of activities "denying the rights of individuals under the constitution." In FBI practice, "extremist" investigations are concerned with extremist groups—the Ku Klux Klan and the Black Panther Party, as well as a variety of terrorist organizations devoted to "guerrilla warfare."

An intelligence organization also faces the constant risk that an informant will overstep himself and become involved personally in an illegal activity—and even that a zealous handling agent will assist him. Robert Hardy managed to infiltrate a group of anti-war activists in Philadelphia in 1970 who planned

to break into the draft board office in neighboring Camden,
New Jersey. Hardy told the Church Committee that he supplied
essential directions and support:

> Everything they learned about breaking into a building or
> climbing a wall or cutting glass or destroying lockers, I
> taught them. I got sample equipment, type of windows
> that we would go through, I . . . taught them how to cut
> the glass, how to drill holes in the glass so you cannot hear
> it, and stuff like that, and the FBI supplied me with the
> equipment needed. The stuff I did not have, the [FBI] got
> off their own agents.

The line is often blurred between what an intelligence agency
terms an "informant" and what the targeted group calls the
detested "informer." Under the latter definition, the informant
informer has a somewhat odious role in history, even from the
viewpoint of the people who used him. As the nineteenth-century British constitutional scholar Sir Thomas May wrote,
"Men may be without restraints upon their liberty; they may
pass to and fro at pleasure: but if their steps are tracked by spies
and informers, their words noted down for crimination, their
associates watched as conspirators—who shall say that they are
free?"

Informers are so reviled in Ireland that contemporary citizens
often shun descendants of persons who betrayed their country-
men to the British two or three centuries previously. When
historian Helen Landreth consulted records for her book *The
Pursuit of Robert Emmet,* she had to sign an agreement not to disclose names of informers she might find in government archives
dating to 1803. The stated reason: to avoid retaliation against
their descendants.

INNERE STADT

The international sector—Fifth District—of Vienna during
the postwar years of occupation by the United States, French,
British, and Soviets. Administrative responsibility and policing
of the *Innere Stadt* rotated on a monthly basis. KGB regarded the
Innere Stadt as a sort of espionage free-fire zone where normal
spying ground rules did not apply. CIA personnel tended to

avoid the *Innere Stadt* unless urgent business required a cautious visit there. Many of KGB's more brutal assassination and kidnapping operations were staged in the *Innere Stadt.*

INSIDE MAN

A CIA case officer who works out of a United States embassy abroad with State Department cover. *(See also* LIGHT COVER; OUTSIDE MAN.)

INSPIRE

To deceive a detected enemy agent into accepting false information and reporting it as truth to his superiors. An agent so deceived is said to be "inspired." Because he is unaware of the "inspiration," he is not the same as a "doubled" agent.

INSURGENCY

A condition resulting from a revolt or insurrection against an established government that falls short of civil war.

INTELLIGENCE

"The product resulting from the collection, evaluation, analysis, integration, and interpretation of all available information that concerns one or more aspects of foreign nations or of areas of operation that is immediately or potentially significant for planning." Such is the definition cited in the *Dictionary of United States Military Terms for Joint Usage,* published by the Department of Army, Navy, and Air Force. Former CIA executive Sherman Kent calls intelligence "the kind of knowledge our state must possess regarding other states in order to assure itself that its cause will not suffer nor its undertakings fail because its statesmen and soldiers plan and act in ignorance."

"Intelligence" can be sub-divided into a multiplicity of sub-categories:

- *Strategic intelligence* is that "required for the formation of policy and military plans and operations at the national and international level."
- *Tactical intelligence* is working-level information about the day-to-day activities of an adversary, particularly in a military context.

- *Combat intelligence* is information for immediate battlefield use.
- *Operational intelligence* is the information required to conduct clandestine espionage missions in a target country.

IN THE NET

A person who has performed an espionage assignment for the KGB, thereby making himself vulnerable to blackmail; witting or not, he now is "owned" by KGB.

INVISIBLE GROUP

Thugs recruited from East German prisons by the East German State Security Service (SSD) and used for strong-arm jobs both by SSD and KGB. Missions ranged from murder to kidnappings and beatings of anti-Communists in West Berlin. The invisible group grabbed or killed scores of prominent anti-Communists during the 1950s; by the computation of West German intelligence, there were 225 abductions and 340 attempted abductions in West Berlin alone during the 1950s. Apolitical for the most part, the invisible group were offered reduced sentences or outright freedom for their efforts. In actuality, after the first mission, they either accepted an "invitation" to become full-time agents or were themselves assassinated.

INTELLIGENCE CYCLE

The steps by which information is assembled, converted into intelligence, and made available to consumers. The cycle is composed of four steps: (1) *direction:* the determination of intelligence requirements, preparation of a collection plan, tasking of collection agencies, and a continuous check on the productivity of these agencies; (2) *collection:* the exploitation of information sources and the delivery of the collected information to the proper intelligence processing unit for use in the production of intelligence; (3) *processing:* the steps whereby information becomes intelligence through evaluation, analysis, integration, and interpretation; and (4) *dissemination:* the distribution of information or intelligence products in oral, written, or graphic form to departmental and agency intelligence consumers. This formidable definition comes from the Church Committee.

At the working level, the intelligence cycle is more succinctly stated, "Get it [information] and get it out."

INTELLIGENCE DATA BASE
All holdings of intelligence data and finished intelligence products at a given department or agency.

ISOLATION
Early CIA cryptonym—or cover name—for the Agency's training facility at Camp Peary, Virginia, on the narrow neck of land between the James and York rivers near Williamsburg, Virginia. In its first years, the purpose of Camp Peary was a fairly well-guarded secret, hence a trainee sent there was said to be in isolation.

IVORY, THE
A small ivory plaque that the British monarch gives to his or her chief of the Secret Service as a token of office; it also supposedly insures swift access in times of emergency.

j

JEDBURGH TEAM, JEDS

The basic intelligence team that entered occupied Europe during World War II, usually by parachute. Each team was composed of an American OSS agent, a British SOE agent, and a member of the French Resistance. At their peak some ninety Jedburgh teams operated in France, coordinating the efforts of resistance groups of thirty to fifty members each. The Jeds disrupted German defenses after the Normandy invasion, blowing up bridges and rail lines and ambushing enemy convoys. The Jeds also operated in Scandinavia.

The teams took their name from their quarters during training—Jedburgh, a royal burgh on the Jed River in the Scots border country of Roxburghshire. According to intelligence historian Anthony Cave Brown, the burgh was "famous for its abbey and infamous for 'Jeddart Justice,' in which a man was hung first and tried afterwards." Among American Jeds was Major William E. Colby, who in 1974 was to become director of Central Intelligence.

JETRO

Acronym for the Japanese External Trade Organization, a government-run international commercial intelligence service whose coverage rivals that of the CIA. JETRO maintains offices in forty-nine countries, including five in the United States; it is concerned mainly with markets and potential U.S. exporters to Japan. JETRO specialists give special attention to computers and other electronic gear that can be pirated and produced at a lower cost in Japan.

JOCK STRAP MEDAL

A decoration awarded to a clandestine operative of CIA. These medals are retained in Agency headquarters until the agent retires, and sometimes forever, if security warrants. The CIA joke is that such medals can be worn "only on your jock strap," since they must be concealed.

JOE

An OSS euphemism for "agent," during the Second World War.

JOINT REPORTS AND RESEARCH UNIT

Cover name for the CIA station in the United States embassy, Grosvenor Square, London; some functions are done by another cover office, the Political Liaison Section.

k

K
Vernacular used by Westerners living in Moscow for an agent (or agents) of the KGB, e.g., "The Ks are following us tonight."

KEEPING BOOKS
The process of keeping rosters of unfriendly intelligence agents operating in one's territory. This is a major chore of the counterespionage sections of CIA stations abroad. CIA routinely compiles a biography of every Soviet diplomat posted abroad (as does KGB of each American diplomat) and Agency counterintelligence specialists are confident of their ability to identify the vast majority of KGB agents working under diplomatic cover.

KEGEBESHNIKI
In-house term by which officers of KGB describe themselves; a contraction of the Russian words in the agency's title.

KEY
Soviet intelligence term for a means or method of persuading a person to work as an agent or informant. In postwar Austria, for instance, the Soviets concentrated on Austrian civilians working in low-level jobs for the American military establishment—cleaners, secretaries, translators, typists, etc. According to the defector A. I. Romanov, "A particularly popular 'key' was to promise an individual that any of his relatives who were prisoners in the USSR would be found and released as quickly as possible. . . . Another way was to obtain work with the Western allies for persons who were known to have pro-Communist views."

KEY INTELLIGENCE REQUIREMENT (KIQ)

Topics of particular interest to national policymakers, as defined by the director of Central Intelligence. KIQs are analogous to the military's EEIs (essential elements of information)

KGB (Komitet Gosudarstvennoe Bezopasnosti)

The Committee for State Security, which MI5, the British counterintelligence service, has called "the biggest spy machine for the gathering of secret information which the world has ever seen." Orwellian in scope, the KGB touches the life of virtually every inhabitant of the USSR. In addition to foreign intelligence functions, KGB runs the internal Soviet police, the censorship system, immigration, and the prisons; it also monitors education, the church, labor, and other organizations. Headquarters are in an ornate, rococo building on a square near the Kremlin named for Felix Dzerzhinsky, the founder of the original USSR security organ that evolved into the KGB. Other Moscow buildings handle overflow: administrative offices in Machovaya Ulitza, and the First Chief Directorate, which handles activities outside the USSR, in a half-moon-shaped building on the ring road around Moscow. KGB calls itself "The Sword and Shield" of the Communist Party.

Soviet intelligence has a dual nature. Its influence abroad, according to David J. Dallin, constitutes "an arm of foreign and military policy, and as such it is comparable to analogous agencies of other powers. It is, however, also part and parcel of the international Communist movement, and in this it is a unique intelligence system." Foreign communists must play both roles. The first statutes of the Communist International, written by Lenin in 1919 (the "twenty-one conditions for admittance"), required that "Communists *everywhere* [emphasis added] are obliged to create a parallel underground apparatus which should help the party to fulfill its duty towards the revolution."

KGB is a lineal descendant of the first Soviet security organization, the *Cheka* (or *Ve Cheka),* founded in 1917. The word comes from the tongue-twisting full Russian title, *Vse-Rossiyskaya Chrezvychaynaya Komissiya Po Borbe S Kontrrevolitisiey I Sabotazhem,* meaning the All-Russian Extraordinary Commission for Combating Counterrevolution and Sabotage. Because of local *Chekas,* the all-Russian or central organization was sometimes called the *Ve Cheka* to distinguish it from the subordinate groups.

Since *Cheka,* Soviet security and intelligence has been known by a succession of names, due to reorganizations and political changes. They are:

- 1922–23: *GPU,* for *Gosudarstvennoe Politicheskoe Upravlenie,* or State Political Administration
- 1923–34: *OGPU,* for *Obedinennoe Gosudarstvennoe Politicheskoe Upravlenye,* or Unified State Political Administration
- 1934–38: *NKVD,* for *Narodnyi Komissariat Vnutrennikh Del,* or People's Commissariat for Internal Affairs
- 1938–46: *NKGB-NKVD,* the former an acronym for *Narodnyi Komissariat Gosudarstvennoe Bezopasnosti* (despite the split of police and security functions, the organization still answered to a single boss, Lavrenti Beria)
- 1946–53: *MVD-MGB,* for the previous agencies, now elevated to ministry level, the *Ministerstvó Gosudarstvennoe Bezospasnosti,* for state security; and the *Ministerstvo Vnutrennikh Del,* for internal affairs
- 1954: *KGB,* the present overall Soviet security police and espionage organization

(See also GRU, KGB BOSSES.)

KGB BOSSES

Felix Dzerzhinsky, the founder of the security police group that became KGB, was a Pole who spent twenty years in the anti-Czarist underground, fighting the *Okhrana,* the royalist secret police. Neither side treated prisoners nicely, and the experience convinced Dzerzhinsky that running a police state was not a job for the squeamish. In a rare press interview in 1917, shortly after the Soviets came to power, "Iron Felix" laid down the operating principles that guided KGB for many decades:

> We stand for organized terror. . . . Terror is the absolute necessity during times of revolution. . . . The Cheka [the organization that eventually became the KGB] is obliged to defend the revolution and conquer the enemy

even if its sword does by chance sometimes fall upon the heads of the innocent.

Despite his reputation for cruelty (he dropped in on tortures with a spectator's enthusiasm), Dzerzhinsky was known to members of his service as "our father." He died in his sleep in 1926.

Vyacheslav Menzhinsky, also a Pole, was a more rational man than Dzerzhinsky, and it was under his auspices the Russian intelligence began fruitful operations abroad. He developed the *Comintern* (the Communist International), an umbrella group that wed Communist parties throughout the world to the USSR, both for political and intelligence purposes. But he fell afoul of Stalin's paranoia, and in 1934 he was poisoned.

Genrikh Yagoda, by most accounts, was the man who administered the poison. Another Pole, he eagerly ran the earliest of Stalin's purges. But in 1937 he was accused of "softness" and put into the dock, where he "admitted" not only that he killed Menzhinsky but also that he was a "foreign agent." Yagoda was taken to the basement of the Lubianka prison and shot.

Nikolai Yezhof, Yagoda's successor, stood only five feet tall, and he deserved his *sotto voce* nickname, "The Bloody Dwarf." In two brisk years, Yezhof (at Stalin's direction) purged not only the Soviet army—killing 90 percent of the general officers and 80 percent of the colonels—but also his own intelligence service. Yezhof was known for impatience; if a prisoner would not talk he would smash a chair, take a jagged fragment, and (with assistance) ram it up the man's rectum. Stalin approvingly called Yezhof "Our Mailed Fist" and "Our Blackberry," both puns on his name in the Russian language. The "Yezovchina"—the Russian term for his reign—rivaled in brutality the worst years of Ivan the Terrible. But he did establish two precedents. He was the first Russian to head Stalin's secret police, and he was the first director to leave the office alive. In 1938 Yezhov was sent off to the position of "Commissar for Inland Waters," and he disappeared from public view. There is scholarly speculation, but no evidence, that Stalin eventually had him shot.

Lavrenti Beria, a Georgian, was Stalin's last and most trusted thug. He took command of the police apparatus in 1938 and controlled it tightly for fifteen years, until his patron's death. Under Beria the NKVD (the then-name for KGB) became veritably a state within a state, managing vast portions of Soviet industry and answering only to Stalin. A squat, beady-eyed sadist, Beria liked to spend slow evenings in the torture chambers of the Lubianka, the KGB prison where events tended to be hard-core.

The British journalist Edward Crankshaw, who reported from Moscow during World War II, described Beria in words that became the arch-description of the Soviet spy boss: ". . . shortish, bald, thick-necked, the face pallid in the Kremlin manner, the nose a little like a duck's bill, but sharp, the mouth tight and thin, the manner gentle and coldly, abstractedly benign—the whole effect of that pedantic aloofness which makes people think of scholars when they should really think of fanatics of the most dangerous kind."

When Stalin died in March 1953, Beria joined the rush to seize the dictator's crown. Such was not to be. His own colleagues distrusted putting such a hoodlum at the head of state. CIA, also wary of a Beria succession, floated a story that he actually had been on the American payroll for years.* In any event, in June 1953 Beria was lured to a Kremlin meeting, where fellow Politburo members seized him and strangled him on the spot. (News of the death was not reported until December 1953, when *Pravda* called him a "foreign agent.")

Sergei Kruglov, who headed the Kremlin security force when Stalin died, had the reputation of a murderer; he was said to have shot personally many of the Red Army officers condemned during the purge trials of the 1930s. Kruglov ran security for the Yalta, Teheran, the Potsdam conferences of the wartime Big Three (Roosevelt, Churchill, and Stalin); for these services, he was made an Honorary Knight of the British Empire and was given the Legion of Merit by the U.S. government, surely the only foreign spymaster ever to wear such awards. After Beria's death, Kruglov ran both the Ministry of the Interior and the Ministry of State Security. But two years later, the Politburo decided no single man should run the entire security

---

* Details of this story—one of the most incredible coups ever achieved by CIA—must await the publication of the memoirs of Hans Tofte, a longtime Agency covert operative. Tofte has told me how he blackened Beria in the Politburo; the full story, however, will best be told by Tofte.

apparatus. So, in 1954, Kruglov was made Minister of the Interior only.

Ivan Aleksandrovich Serov, who became Secretary of State Security, was an unrepentant Stalinist and also a Beria deputy; that he continued in power was taken as evidence that the new Kremlin leadership did not yet dare challenge KGB as an institution. Serov's power base was his friendship with Premier Nikita Khrushchev, with whom he had first worked closely in 1938 in the Ukraine. Serov properly blooded himself in the secret police by directing the murder of scores of thousands of civilians in the Baltic states during World War II.

A busy man socially, Serov in his prime was well known to Westerners in Moscow—although some thought it amusing that he continued to wear the thick-soled shoes that lesser KGB thugs consider part of their uniform. Oleg Penkovskiy, who had frequent contact with Serov while working simultaneously for CIA and GRU, described him as "not the most brilliant of men. He knows how to interrogate people, imprison them, and shoot them." When Serov accompanied Khrushchev to London in 1955, the press denounced him as a "butcher, odious thug and grinning gunman." The criticism so outraged Serov that he stormed back to Moscow.

But Serov thrived on brute force. He personally led the KGB goon squad that broke into a Moscow banquet hall the night of November 3, 1956, and hauled a delegation of Hungarian officials away from a supposed "state dinner." Hungarian Defense Minister Pal Maleter, who had run the recent uprising in his country and then been lured to Moscow on a pretext, was among those arrested; he was shot. Serov fell from power in 1959 with disclosure that a longtime KGB official, Pyotr Popov, had worked as a CIA mole.

Aleksandr N. Shelepin, the next KGB boss, was only forty years of age when he assumed power in 1959 after a career in the *Komosol,* the Communist youth organization, and as a leader in what passes for Soviet "labor organizations." Shelepin stands as the only intelligence chief in recent history to publicly acclaim an assassin. The honoree was Bogdan Stashinsky, who murdered two exile dissidents in Western Europe in 1957 and 1959. After the second killing, Shelepin summoned Stashinsky to KGB headquarters and—in the name of the Presidium of the Supreme Soviet, as the Politburo was then known—awarded him the Order of the Red Banner. Shelepin left KGB in 1961 to run the Soviet labor confederation.

Vladimir Semichastny was also young when he took the helm, only forty-three, and he was scarcely known even within the USSR bureaucracy. Some analysts have suggested Khrushchev wished just such a nondescript man running KGB during his consolidation of power in the USSR. Semichastny attracted public attention only once. When Boris Pasternak won the Nobel Prize for literature, Semichastny called him a "pig." Pasternak smiled. But Semichastny, with his policeman's dogged dedication to files, did embarrass his service and his country—and Khrushchev—in his bungled handling of the case of Frederick Baaghoorn, a Yale professor. Because Baaghoorn had served in the State Department during the war, KGB drones convinced themselves he must be a spy when he came to the USSR on a research trip. They arrested him on trumped-up charges at the Metropole Hotel in 1963 and then tried to trade him for a low-level Amtorg chauffeur caught spying in New York. President Kennedy made a personal issue of the case, and Khrushchev had to free Baaghoorn. Semichastny lasted another four years, but quietly out of sight.

Yuri Vladimirovich Andropov was the KGB chief best known to the West because he ultimately became Soviet premier. He also enjoyed perhaps the best press of any chief ever. A thin man with scholarly demeanor, Andropov certainly appeared more benign than the scowling Beria. Further, he was not a professional KGB man. He spent his career as a bureaucrat and diplomat before taking charge of KGB in 1967. But he earned his bloody spurs: In 1956, for instance, as ambassador to Budapest, Andropov worked with Serov in betraying supposed "allies" to grisly deaths.

Thus Andropov adjusted well to the cynical realities of KGBdom. He pioneered the use of "psychiatric" treatment of dissidents; he slammed the door on Jews trying to flee a nation that did not want them; he was surrogate paymaster to uncountable international terrorists who did KGB's bidding. But when Andropov succeeded Leonid Brezhnev as premier in late 1982, these cruelties had to be explained away.

Cleansing a KGB director to make him fit as chief of state is on its face an impossible task; even the most cursory of glances spots the thousands of crushed lives in Andropov's wake.

Nonetheless, KGB disinformation worked to scrub the blood off Andropov's sword. The naive American press helped. The *Washington Post,* one of the more gullible accomplices, called Andropov a "well-educated and enlightened man—even a closet liberal—despite the stigma . . . as head of the KGB." One former CIA officer commented, "Calling Andropov a 'closet liberal' is akin to calling Jack the Ripper an 'alley liberal' because that's where he killed his victims."

Vitaly V. Fedorchuk, Andropov's successor, held office only seven months—from May through December 1982—before moving on to the more sensitive job of Minister of Internal Affairs. Fedorchuk is one of the rare KGB chiefs to have done intelligence work abroad. A native of the Ukraine, Fedorchuk served in the Red Army during the war, then was assigned to East Germany as head of KGB's "Directorate of Special Departments." This unit bore responsibility for peacetime kidnappings, killings, and sabotage. His mettle proved, Fedorchuk returned to his native Ukraine as KGB regional chief in 1970, at a time of swelling nationalist unrest. In the words of Soviet expert Adrian Karatnycky, "In 1972, he orchestrated the most severe wave of political arrests and repressions to have occurred anywhere in the USSR in the post-Stalin era." Fedorchuk purged Ukraine party boss Petro Shelest and thousands of his adherents; KGB became the *de facto* government of the Ukraine. At the end of the decade, Karatnycky has written, Ukrainian political prisoners accounted for "over 40 percent of the Soviet Union's known political prisoners; nearly two-and-a-half times the proportion of Ukrainians in the Soviet population." Fedorchuk effectively scotched any idea of Polish labor dissidents finding support in the Western U.S.S.R.

Viktor M. Chebrikov, a metallurgist by training, a career KGBnik by trade, had the fortune to be close both to Brezhnev (he is from Denpropetrovsk, where Brezhnev once was party boss) and to Andropov. His first major KGB post, in 1967, was personnel chief; a year later, he became one of six deputy directors. Chebrikov keeps low; when CIA analysts scurried for information about their new adversary, they found only twelve lines about him in the official USSR government yearbook.

The fact that its leaders historically lacked any hands-on experience in real espionage has not deterred KGB from aggressively challenging the West, through disinformation, active measures, support of terrorists and thefts of technological and other intelligence. The conclusion of Western analysts is that KGB is now so institutionalized as an apparatus that a change of leadership does not affect its ongoing foreign operations. The director is significant only in terms of internal Soviet and party politics; he remains a security policeman first and foremost hence the KGB's power.

Kh. V. (Khranit' vechno)

Russian words for "to be kept in perpetuity." Intelligence files to be so maintained bear the *Kh. V.* stamp. But the words are rarely spoken directly by insiders. The prefer the obtuse words, *"Khristos voskresye,"* an Eastern greeting exchanged by Orthodox Christians after a church service. When spoken by one Soviet intelligence officer to another, the words had no religious meaning; however, their first letters, *"Kh. v.,"* signaled that the files being discussed were to be retained permanently.

KING GEORGE'S CAVALRY

A British term meaning, in effect, when all other efforts fail, buy what you need ("Send in King George's Cavalry").

KNUCKLE DRAGGER

A paramilitary soldier working for CIA. The term began as a derogatory one—that the "paras" (usually military men detached to Agency duty) were "such apes that their knuckles drag the ground when they walk." But one can now use the word to a "para" without expecting a punch in the mouth.

KONTORA GRUBYKH BANDITOV

Russian for "Office of Crude Bandits," a play on KGB's real title, *Komitet Gosudarstvennoy Bezopasnosti,* or "Committee for State Security." This is an inside joke among KGB officers and would not be heard from the Soviet man-in-the-street. KGB has no illusions about the nature of its work and discuss it with cynicism—among themselves, but not with outsiders.

KREMLIN KOMMANDANT (KK)

A KGB section answerable only to the head of the Soviet Union—a personal inspectorate of "spies who watch the spies." Agents assigned to the KK must swear an oath of allegiance to the Politboro. The KK supervises Kremlin security as well.

1

"L" Pill

The so-called "suicide capsule" carried by British and American agents during World War II, a lethal dose of cyanide encased in glass. Concealed in a false tooth, the "L" pill could be worked free by the agent's tongue; a sharp bite was required to break the glass, with death following quickly. If the agent accidentally swallowed the pill—say, during his sleep—it would pass through his body unbroken and harmless. Persons liable to capture who know of such top secret plans as the Normandy invasion were fitted with an "L" pill.

LEAGUE OF FREE JURISTS

A lawyer-oriented group founded in West Germany in the late 1940s to wage political warfare against the puppet East German government, and to facilitate escapes from behind the Iron Curtain. UJF (the initials for its German name) was supported, but not controlled, by CIA. Its greatest strength was advice on how East Germans could avoid—if not circumvent entirely—new Communist laws restricting the economy. UJF kept a close watch on misconduct of East German lawyers and police, with the stated aim of justice once Communism was overthrown. With the detente of the 1960s, UJF ceased to be a significant force.

LEAK

The deliberate or accidental disclosure of classified information. In the current Washington sense, the former is most often the reason: officials in government leak secrets in order to advance their programs or damage those of bureaucratic rivals.

In the intelligence context, a leak is apt to come from a loose-tongued person who cannot resist bragging about the importance of his work, often after being encouraged by Eros, ego, or John Barleycorn. The existence of such blabbermouths means that low-level counterintelligence functionaries spend an inordinate amount of time hanging around bars and restaurants near sensitive installations, listening for persons who should know better.

Despite the understandable human thirst for "inside" information, wary Washington officials occasionally shut themselves off from disclosures of classified material for fear they might inadvertently leak it. For instance, in 1961, the director of Central Intelligence, Allen Dulles, tried to brief Postmaster General J. Edward Day on CIA mail intercept programs, prefacing his remarks with the comment that "he wanted to tell me something very secret." Do I have to know about it? Day asked. "No," replied Dulles. Whereupon Day stated, "My experience is that where there is something that is very secret, it is likely to leak out, and anybody that knew about it is likely to be suspected of having been part of leaking it, so I would rather not know anything about it."

The word "leak" put a new term into the American political lexicon in the early 1970s. Irked by disclosures of several sensitive items (notably the American bombings of Vietcong installations in Cambodia), the Nixon White House created a special unit to try to contain the leaks. E. Howard Hunt, the former CIA officer in charge of the office, promptly termed his operation "The Plumbers."

LEGAL

An intelligence officer who works abroad with no attempt to conceal his nationality. But his actual work usually is by no means legal under laws of his host country. The legal is attached to the embassy or to another open activity of his government. But his cover job shrouds his true mission. KGB legals make up the bulk of any embassy staff in Western countries. Even when expelled for "activities incompatible with diplomatic status," these spies are never acknowledged as intelligence officers. The official position of the United States government is that the State Department has "an unyielding policy against the issuance of false passports or, indeed, their use by official or unofficial personnel under any circumstances." Such was written, supposedly with a straight face, by long-time CIA officer Kermit Roosevelt in his 1979 book, *Countercoup.* Roosevelt's statement does not jibe with my first-hand knowledge of the use of American passports abroad.

A legal who uses diplomatic cover has immunity from arrest. His true identity is presumed to be known by the other side. An "open" legal will not be directly involved in espionage himself —common sense says he will be under surveillance—but he will keep in frequent contact with the ranking resident clandestine agent. As British journalist Stephen Stewart has described the legal, "His function is to effect exchanges, to receive warnings from the host country about the activities of his resident, and generally to help undo the cumbersome tangles which any espionage service leaves in its wake."

The Soviets enhance their number of legals through use of the United Nations and other international organizations. Although sworn to work as international civil servants rather than in the interest of the USSR, the Soviets do no such thing. Arkady N. Shevchenko, Undersecretary of the UN until he defected in 1978, has written, "It is probably no exaggeration to count over half of the more than seven hundred Soviets in New York City as either full-time spies or co-opts under KGB or GRU orders or influence." In the political section of the Soviet Mission to the UN itself, at one time no less than twenty-one of twenty-eight "diplomats" worked either for KGB or GRU, Shevchenko stated.

LEGAT

Cable abbreviation for "legal attaché," the not-so-secret title used by FBI agents assigned to American embassies abroad. Legats first appeared in Latin America just before World War II, when FBI Director J. Edgar Hoover sought to build a bureaucratic fence to keep out the archrival Office of Strategic Services. As matters worked out the FBI, and not the OSS, had counterintelligence responsibility in Latin America for the duration of the war. Hoover thereafter began implanting his legats in embassies worldwide. Their prime function today is liaison between local law enforcement agencies and their American counterparts. In some instances the legat might even be a non-FBI person; in Spain, for instance, the Drug Enforcement

Agency has at times held the position. Legats are often pestered by traveling American businessmen in pursuit of advice on local legal matters. These persons are politely shunted to a commercial attaché.

LEGEND

The elaborate (if bogus), "biography" an intelligence agency prepares for an agent who is to be dispatched abroad with an assumed identity. The depth and verifiability of the legend depends upon the sensitivity of the mission. The legend disguises the agent's true background and gives him a plausible reason for living in the new country. The KGB historically has liked to use Russians disguised as Canadians born of émigré parents, who then move to the United States.

LEGITIMATE

CIA word for an outsider—a businessman or a journalist—who is exactly what he purports to be, and not living under a cover story. ("Oh, he's legitimate.") A legitimate is unwittingly useful to a CIA station because he can occupy the attention of surveillance teams that might otherwise be pestering actual agents. For mischief, an embassy political officer might dine publicly with a legitimate to further the conception that the visitor is an intelligence officer, thereby stimulating interest in his movements. This raises certain risks, the least of which is that the legitimate might have trouble obtaining a visa when next he tries to enter the country.

LETTER-DROP

A location where an agent can leave a secret communication to be retrieved by his control, or by another agent. A good letter-drop must have contradictory features. It should be in a busy enough area that a stroller is not conspicuous. Yet it also should be secure enough that the message does not fall into the wrong hands. Further, security demands that some time lapse between the deposit of a message in the letter-drop and its retrieval. The sorts of drops used by Western and rival intelligence agencies during the past decades form an endless list: from loose stones in fences in Central Park in New York to radiators in Moscow apartment foyers to toilet tanks in the United States Capitol.

The person who leaves a message in a drop so indicates by a visible signal posted elsewhere—a chalk mark on a wall, a thumb-tack on a park bench, even a piece of adhesive tape on a particular post in the esplanade on F Street Northwest behind the National Press Building in Washington (a KGB signal for several months in the late 1960s). The retrieval agent does not go to the drop until the signal tells him that it is "loaded."

According to Soviet expert William Hood, formerly of CIA, public telephone booths are favored drops for KGB. *(See also* DEAD DROP BOX.)

LIGHT COVER

The use of diplomatic credentials by a CIA officer stationed abroad. Such an agent identifies himself as an "American official" or "embassy staff" without elaboration. Most officers with light cover at the outset make their true positions known only to local security officials with whom they have contact. But word eventually gets around to most everyone else of substance in the capital. In Soviet Bloc countries an officer under light cover is considered the lightning rod who attracts potential defectors who need access to CIA in a hurry. He is also the accepted contact in the event the agency of the "host" country desires to discuss professional ground rules about the conduct of agents.

LIGHTNING BOLT (blyskawica)

Vernacular among Polish intelligence attachés and code clerks for a top priority message.

LIMPET

A magnetized device that can be attached to a piece of metal —such as the underside of a toilet tank—to pass along a message at a drop. Good trade-craft calls for the agent who makes the pickup to carry away the limpet and dispose of it discreetly; leaving it in place risks accidental discovery.

LINECROSSERS

Army military intelligence term for low-level agents who are sent behind enemy lines in a combat situation. These persons are particularly valuable when the area they enter is part of their homeland, occupied by enemy troops. The U.S. Army's Counterintelligence Corps made wide use of linecrossers during the Korean War. So, too, did CIA, which managed to infiltrate South Korean linecrossers into the big Soviet naval base at Vladivostok. (*See also* BORDER CROSSERS.)

LITERARY SPOOKS

Despite the desired secrecy of espionage and good intelligence work, the spy trade has long attracted men of letters, both journalists and more serious writers. Many kept quiet about their activities; others did not, and built literary careers upon their clandestine experiences. The most famous "quiet spy" was Daniel Defoe, author of *Robinson Crusoe* and many other works, who worked extensively on covert missions for the British Crown, yet wrote not a word about his activities. Undoubtedly there are others of more recent vintage, and perhaps history ultimately will reveal them.

Intelligence services of all nations recruit journalists as either full-time agents or casual informants, for obvious reasons. Journalists have easy access to important officials who do not always guard their tongues when speaking to a newsman, and, of course, the nature of their work provides an excellent cover for clandestine activities. Chapman Pincher, the veteran British writer and espionage specialist, records that Soviet intelligence was particularly anxious to recruit journalists during the 1930s. Similarly, many prominent intelligence figures worked as newsmen before turning to spying for their own countries. Roger Hollis, wartime head of MI5, worked in China during the 1920s as a stringer for the *South China Times* and then for the *Peking Times;* oddly, both papers were anti-British at the time. Kim Philby worked as a correspondent for *The Times* of London before joining MI6; simultaneously with his newspaper duties, he worked as a Soviet agent. After his exposure, he worked as a correspondent for *The Economist* in the 1960s, based in Beirut. Richard Helms's first job, after graduating from Williams College in 1935, was as a United Press correspondent in Europe; a minor coup was an interview with Hitler. Helms was to become director of Central Intelligence three decades later.

LITERARY CHUTZPAH

In 1929 the Soviet writer N. G. Smirnov published a novel, *The Diary of a Spy*, the central character of which was a cold-blooded and ruthless but most successful British spy named Edward Kent. Victor Sukulov, a Red Army officer and intelligence trainee, was so smitten with the book—and the glamorous Englishman—that he adopted "Kent" as his legend name. When he began to rise through intelligence ranks, wiser persons counseled that the name attracted undue attention, and he was persuaded to abandon it. Sukulov's choice, in retrospect, makes about as much sense as an MI5 fledgling insisting on being called James Bond.

THE BOND MYSTIQUE, PRO AND CON

Ian Fleming, a former officer of the British Secret Intelligence Service, wrote several competent but modestly received spy books about James Bond, Agent 007, during the late 1950s. Soon after his election, President Kennedy mentioned that Fleming was his favorite "escape reading" author, an unsolicited accolade that made Fleming a very rich man. But despite his popularity with Kennedy, James Bond was considered with disdain by intelligence professionals, chiefly because of his reliance upon whiz-bang gadgetry. The British agent Greville Wynne, while being transported by the KGB from Hungary to the USSR via a military aircraft, decided that escape was impossible. But he mused, "I suppose that James Bond would have spat from his mouth a gas capsule (concealed in his molar) which would have overcome everyone but himself and would then have leapt to safety with a parachute concealed up his backside. But I regret that the British Intelligence Service lags behind Bond in ingenuity."

Somerset Maugham, an SIS agent in Geneva during World War I, perhaps prefigured Bond's high-life spying in his novel *Ashenden,* about a British agent. As one of Maugham's agents poured himself a snifter of brandy, he remarked, "In my youth, I was always taught that you should take a woman by the waist and a bottle by the neck."

GHOST WRITERS IN THE SPIES

Once an intelligence agency debriefs a defector, it often exacts further value from him by encouraging the writing of a "memoir." Such accounts contain much useful and accurate material; nonetheless, they must be read with caution, and the foreknowledge that ultimate editorial control is wielded by an intelligence agency. Kim Philby did double duty for the KGB after fleeing to Moscow. First came his own *My Silent War*, chockful of both misinformation and outright mischief (unfounded slurs against former SIS colleagues, chiefly). Philby persuaded his old friend Graham Greene to write a foreword for the book; despite the prestige lent by Greene's name, *My Silent War* was dismissed by serious readers as silly propaganda. Yuri Andropov, then head of KGB, "encouraged" Philby also to help fellow spy Gordon Lonsdale write his memoir, *Spy: Twenty Years of Secret Service*.

The West has its own ghostwriters. *Handbook for Spies*, ostensibly by the defected Soviet agent Alexander Foote, actually was written by MI5 officer Courtney Young, case officer for the turned agent. Young carefully peppered the book with disinformation to mislead the Soviets as to exactly what Foote had told MI5 about Russian intelligence.

SPOOKONYMS

For various reasons, many persons who write about espionage do so under pen names. Herewith a sampling of some of the more prominent:

E. Howard Hunt, former CIA officer	Robert Dietrich, John Baxter, Gordon Davis, David St. John
Edward Spiro, former Czech resistance fighter	E. H. Cookridge
James MacCargar, former CIA officer	Christopher Felix
Rupert Allason	Nigel West
Donald McCormick	Richard Deacon
André Lèon Brouillard	Pierre Nord
Richard Henry Michael Clayton	William Haggard

David John Moore Cornwell	John le Carré
John Creasy	J. H. Marric, Michael Halliday, Gordon Ashe, Anthony Morton, Norman Deane, Jeremy York, among undisclosed others, for a total 562 books.
John Innes McIntosh Stewart	Michael Innes
Kingsley Amis	Robert Markham
Alistair Maclean	Ian Stuart

LITMUS TEST

A counterintelligence trick intended to put false information before a suspected informer or agent and to monitor the results. For instance, the suspect might be told that a prospective Soviet defector intends to meet an agent at a certain location at a set time. Surveillance teams flood the area (discreetly) to see if any KGB agents show up to monitor the meeting. Another variation is to give false information to a suspect and then see if it shows up in unfriendly hands or is mentioned in radio traffic from the local Soviet embassy.

LIVE LETTER BOXES

Subagents who willingly or unwittingly pass messages to other persons. For instance, he or she might be asked to drop off a parcel at a specific address, or to post a letter from a distant city while traveling.

LIVE LETTER-DROPS (LLDs)

A low-level operative recruited to receive letters and forward them to a case officer. According to long-time CIA agent William Hood, persons who seldom travel and who receive so little mail that they are unlikely to confuse personal letters with spy correspondence are the best LLDs. Traffic is slow—perhaps as little as one letter every year or two—so the case officer will sometimes mail "dummy letters" to insure that the drop is operative.

LIVE TAP

A telephone tap that is monitored by a listener, rather than being recorded for later study. Live taps are used sparingly, given their high manpower cost. An example: The FBI suspects that a Czech spy is about to leave the United States, and it wishes to stay informed of his airline reservations. Thus an agent will put a tap on his home telephone and listen to all conversations, so that arrest teams can be ready.

LOCK STUDIES

A special course for FBI agents chosen for "black bag jobs"; essentially, instruction in how to pick locks and open safes. The courses were conducted at the bureau laboratory in Washington. *(See also* DAME.)

LOG SUMMARIES

The notes an FBI wiretap team compiles during a shift of listening to telephone conversations. The calls themselves are tape-recorded. The listening agent adds "supplementary notes" concerning the identities of the speaking parties and the subject of the conversation, if unclear from the tape. But because of the lack of specific instructions, the Church Committee noted, "the summaries tended to be over-inclusive rather than under-inclusive; the supervising agent noted, for instance, that any information obtained about the subject's sex life or drug use would usually be included in the log summaries."

LONDON CAGE (KPM)

A rather rough interrogation center the British set up at 6-7 Kensington Palace Gardens, London, for the questioning of major Nazi criminals after World War II. Key figures of the Abwehr, or German military intelligence service, were processed through London Cage. The camp was directed by Lieutenant Colonel Alexander Patterson Scotland, a native of South West Africa who joined the German Army to protest British colonialism (the British and the Germans contested control of his homeland), then in disgust went to British intelligence. His background made Scotland a formidable adversary.

THE LONG MARCH THROUGH THE INSTITUTIONS

Soviet intelligence's ongoing attempt to infiltrate and influence the British "establishment," beginning in the early 1930s by planting long-term "moles" in such places as the Foreign Office and other Whitehall departments, media centers such as *The Times* and the British Broadcasting Corporation, the unions, and apparently even the Church of England. Michael Straight, an American who was recruited as a Soviet agent while at Cambridge, used the term in his 1960s confession to the FBI. Just how far the Soviets got on their "long march" is still a subject of heated debate in British intelligence circles. British intelligence writer Chapman Pincher first brought the term to public notice.

LONG VIEW PUBLISHING COMPANY, INC.

Publishing arm of the Communist Party, U.S.A. Based at 239 West 23d Street, New York (also the CPUSA national office), Long View publishes such Communist periodicals as the *Daily World*, successor to the *Daily Worker*, and *Voz del Pueblo*, a "workers' paper" in Spanish. Anything with the Long View imprimatur is slavishly subservient to the Moscow line. A curious citizen who sends one dollar to Long View for a trial subscription to the *Daily World* might receive the five-times weekly newspaper for years on end; journalistic nonsense, the paper is nonetheless valuable in that it announces Soviet disinformation themes in more or less literate English.

THE LOOT

Information obtained through an intelligence operation. (From the French gangster term, *"le grisbi."*)

LUBIANKA

The prison section of KGB headquarters at 2 Dzerzhinsky Square, two blocks from the Kremlin. In pre-revolutionary Russia, Lubianka was the name of the entire complex of buildings. The square was dominated by two insurance companies, "Russia" and "Anchor." A single Soviet insurance company succeeded them, known by the acronym *Gosstrakh*, from the words *gosudarstvennoye* and *strakhovanive*. The first word means "state"; the second, "insurance." But in Russian, the word *strakh*, the last syllable of the acronym, means "terror." So, in Russian jest, the complex has gone from "state insurance" to "state terror."

Uncountable thousands of persons have been imprisoned and executed in Lubianka, including at least three deposed chiefs of the secret police. From the testimony of the few prisoners who came out of Lubianka in condition to tell their stories, the first exposure to the brutal, grim prison is a shock, regardless of what they *thought* they knew of conditions there. Greville Wynne, the British businessman who was a major Western contact with Oleg Penkovskiy, remembered an "elevator within an elevator," into which he was squeezed in a standing position, his face pressed against a small peephole. The elevator descent —"down, down, down"—lasted "probably less than a minute, but it seemed like an eternity. That slow sinking journey was the end of my life. . . ."

m

MAD (Militärischer Abschirmdienst)

West German military counterintelligence, the "Military Screening Service." Comparable in function to the U.S. Army's CIC, charged with protecting the West German armed forces *(Bundeswehr)* from espionage and subversive activities.

MAIL COVER

A request to the U.S. Postal Service, by an intelligence or law enforcement agency, to examine the exterior of mail addressed to or from a particular individual or organization. The mail itself is not opened. The person or organization is not made aware of the cover.

MAIN ENEMY

A widely used translation of the Russian term *glavnyy protivnik,* which can also be read as "main opponent" or "main adversary." By whatever translation, the *glavnyy protivnik* of KGB is the United States. But in GRU usage, oddly, the translation takes another twist: to *probable* enemy. When a Western interrogator is talking with a captured spy, and is uncertain which of the services he owes loyalty to, whether the spy uses "main enemy" or "probable enemy" can be significant.

MAKE

When a person under intelligence surveillance identifies his followers, he "makes" them. An identified surveillant is "made."

MAKING A PASS

The physical handing of a message to a courier or agent.

MALINA
The Russian term for SAFE HOUSE.

MAYDAY BOOK
A detailed book listing the exact procedures to be followed in the event an agent in the field suspects that he is about to be arrested. The Mayday book—a term borrowed from the airlines and shipping—is available to a duty officer at all times, and persons who could be responsible for extricating the agent from danger must be reachable by telephone at any hour. The agent activates the emergency procedures by speaking a coded phrase over the telephone. He is instructed to dial a telephone number that is used for no other purpose (one can imagine a panicked agent receiving a busy signal) and that is tested at least once daily to insure that it is in working order.

MEASLES
A killing done so discreetly that death appears to stem from natural causes. KGB poison needles were a prime source of "measles" during the early Cold War years.

MEMUNEH
Title given the head of Mossad, the Israeli intelligence service, who by law cannot be named publicly during his service.

MERCURY LOADS
Pistol slugs containing a dot of mercury, which causes a drastic increase in penetration of and damage to the target. A tool of a professional assassin. A mercury load will enable .22-caliber long-rifle round to gouge a huge chunk out of concrete—or to destroy much of a victim's head.

MfS (Ministerium für Stastssicherheit)
The East German Ministry for State Security, run by KGB. According to two KGB defectors, the *MfS* is "Russian through the top three layers," although East Germans appear in the nominal hierarchy. Because of their low esteem, *MfS* officers are known as "eminently purchasable" by Western agencies. But they are seldom "purchased," because, as one former CIA of-

ficer states, "They carry K-Mart goods, nothing of value." (He referred to the cut-rate American discount house, and he meant that the *MfS* defectors to date were not worth the processing effort.)

MI5

Great Britain's internal security organization, responsible for counterespionage and counterintelligence within the United Kingdom. Also known as the "Security Service." As was stated by a Crown Minister in 1945, when the government was deciding upon MI5's postwar role, "The purpose of the Security Service is the defense of the Realm, and nothing else." MI5 has suffered so many security scandals the past three decades that it has a dubious reputation among fellow agencies. John le Carré used MI5 as the basis for his Smiley novels, and renamed it "The Circus." Address mail to Room 055, The War Office, London.

MI6

Great Britain's overseas intelligence organization, also known as the "Secret Intelligence Service," or SIS. Roughly comparable in function to America's CIA. Once the world's premier intelligence service, MI6 has declined along with the rest of the British Empire. In the opinion of many professions, its only accomplishment the past two decades was to provide a background for the James Bond espionage novels. MI6's main offices are in Century House, Number 100 Westminster Bridge Road, London —with a Mobil Oil gasoline station occupying the ground floor.

MICE

CIA acronym used to summarize the four most common motives for the defection of a KGB functionary: Money, Ideology, Compromise, and Ego.

MICRODOT

A German technical development that put British intelligence into a tizzy the first days of World War II. A document was photographed through a camera, similar to a *reversed* high-powered microscope, onto a special film that had virtually no grain. The result was a *micropunkt:* a small, shiny full-stop negative from which could be read, through a microscope used in the ordinary way, the text of an entire document. Ewen Montagu of British intelligence said the microdot process, when discovered, "was terrifying to our security people." The dot could be pasted over any period in a book or a newspaper or letter, almost impossible to detect by casual observation. Given the flood of mail that went through Allied censorship stations, the possibilities for espionage use of the dots were endless. Fortunately for the Allies, the Germans' use of the microdots was limited by their inability to supply field agents with the necessary cameras.

MICROPUNKT

German for microdot. *(See also* MICRODOT.)

MIGHTY WURLITZER

A CIA program in which stories were planted in either controlled or friendly publications outside the United States and then reprinted elsewhere, with the aim of either discrediting the Soviet Union or calling attention to an incident the United States wished to publicize. For instance, a writer on a British newspaper would be given a true summary of a problem in Soviet agriculture. The printing of the story in his newspaper gave it further legitimacy, and it could then be circulated by such aboveboard agencies as the United States Information Service. USIS officers could simply hand the printed item to local editors and say, "This is what the *Times* of London said last week; you might find it of interest."

Frank Wisner, one of America's more renowned operatives of the postwar period, is credited for originating—and naming—the Mighty Wurlitzer. Signs of the Wurlitzer's continued existence are visible to close readers of the foreign press, but CIA people no longer boast about it, even *sotto voce.*

MIKETEL

An ordinary telephone that has been converted (clandestinely) into an open microphone capable of intercepting all conversations within hearing range—even when the telephone is not in use. A minute transmitter is planted in the mouthpiece of the telephone. A remote beeper signal, transmitted by a conventional telephone call, activates the transmitters (but without making the phone itself ring). The transmitter is powered by the current within the telephone system; hence no battery or other external power source is required. The person doing the bugging simply listens on the telephone to the conversation in the vicinity of the wired phone, or attaches a tape recorder so that he may review what is said at his leisure. One company advertised its version of the miketel as a "Coast-to-Coast Room Bug Transmitter." Another called the device the "Tele-Ear," and cautioned in its ads:

WARNING!
THE TELE-EAR IS NOT A "BUG"!

Because the very nature of this fantastic device makes it possible to monitor areas without observance, we must point out that federal law permits the use of the TELE-EAR *ONLY* as a burglar alarm.

It is illegal to use the TELE-EAR to surreptitiously monitor the conversations of parties that are unaware of its presence!

MINIMAX FIRE EXTINGUISHER COMPANY

Cover name for the London office of the Secret Intelligence Service in Broadway Buildings, 54 Broadway, opposite the St. James's Park Underground station, during the first months of World War II. Later the brass plaque with the Minimax name was supplemented by another sign, "Government Communications Department." (Today the old SIS offices are occupied by the legal and public health divisions of the Thames Water Authority.)

MISCHIEF, INCORPORATED

Left-wing British euphemism for "MI," the formal designation for Great Britain's two major intelligence services, MI5 and MI6.

MOBILE BRIGADES, MOBILE GROUPS

The special units used by Soviet intelligence for executions of "state enemies" abroad. According to one-time Soviet agent Alexander Orlov, "The decision to perform an 'execution' abroad, a rather risky affair, was up to Stalin personally. . . . It was too dangerous to operate through local agents, who might 'deviate' later and start to talk." Hence the use of what Orlov called mobile brigades.

MOLE

A high-level penetration agent who can give the innermost secrets of an intelligence service to its enemy. The most famed mole in espionage history was H. A. R. "Kim" Philby, who rose to the top of British counterintelligence while working as a Soviet agent. (For more on moles and the term's origin, see the Introduction.)

MODI'IN

Israel's military intelligence service.

MONEY

A principle of intelligence is that an agent *must* be paid, regardless of the depth of his ideological motivation. But the approach is dictated by the nature of the person. If he is an out-and-out rogue, willing to betray his country or another, the questions to be resolved are "How much?" and "How?" The "idealistic" agent is first persuaded to accept expenses, then "payment for your time." KGB is especially strict in enforcing the pay principle. As David J. Dallin has written, "An agent who works without pay feels independent and can give up his spying activities whenever he desires; he might reconsider his decision and reveal his activities to the authorities, minimizing his guilt by stressing his 'idealistic motives.' A paid agent, however modest his remuneration, is a *serving* person, a subordinate, a dependent individual. He is expected to be humble, obedient, and silent; his decisions and moves must be discussed and approved before he can take any action; receipts bearing his signature can be produced and used to coerce him if he should desert the Soviet service. He is firmly in the hands of his employer." Even Sam Carr, the Canadian Communist who worked for GRU until exposed by Igor Gouzenko in 1946, was not averse to putting Soviet money in his pocket, his ideology notwithstanding; as his "control card" noted, "financially secure but takes money."

Earl Browder, head of the American Communist Party, and active in espionage, took such gifts as Russian caviar and bottles of Scotch; his wife liked Russian cognac; his brother Bill had a thirst for Soviet-purchased Canadian Club whiskey.

When Whittaker Chambers protested to his Soviet superior about giving gifts to persons who were "Communists on principle," the superior replied, "Who pays is boss, and who takes money must also give something." When Chambers warned "you will lose every one of them," the superior replied, "Then we must give them some costly present so that they will know that they are dealing with big, important people." One of the persons eventually receiving a handsome rug that year was Alger Hiss, who years later was convicted of perjury for denying involvement in Soviet espionage. The Christmas rug was part of the evidence used to prove Hiss's guilt.

MONGOOSE, OPERATION

The action that President John F. Kennedy directed CIA to undertake in November 1961 "to help Cuba overthrow the Communist regime" in Cuba. MONGOOSE eventually included such actions as simple intelligence and propaganda operations; sabotage of factories and bombings of power lines; spreading nonlethal chemicals in sugar fields to sicken cane cutters; and plots to murder Premier Fidel Castro. Although CIA was to receive public and Congressional criticism for MONGOOSE, the prime mover was President Kennedy; CIA acted on his direct orders.

MOONLIGHT EXTRADITION

The extralegal deportation of a person sought for intelligence or law enforcement purposes. He is arrested by police of a friendly state and delivered across a border without the bother of judicial procedures. A good example: in 1949, Soviet atomic spy Morton Sobell, alerted of his impending arrest, fled to Mexico in expectation of taking a freighter to Eastern Europe. But Mexican police working with the FBI grabbed him in a Gulf

Coast city and drove him nonstop to the Texas border, where he was handed over to American authorities without benefit of formal extradition. Since Sobell had entered Mexico under a false name, he had no appellate recourse.

MOONSHINE

An electronic device, circa World War II, used to amplify and return the pulses of German radar and thus simulate large numbers of approaching ships or aircraft.

MORALE OPERATIONS

A branch of the OSS that had perhaps the broadest mandate for creative mischief in the history of warfare. As stated in an OSS authorization manual, these operations encompassed "all measures of subversion other than physical used to create confusion and diversion, and to undermine the morale and the political unity of the enemy through any means, operating within or purporting to operate within enemy countries and enemy-occupied or controlled countries, and from bases within other areas, including neutral areas, where action or counteraction may be effective against the enemy."

Morale Operations' objectives were "to incite and spread dissension, confusion and disorder; to promote subversive activities against his [the enemy's] government by encouraging underground groups, and to depress the morale of his people . . . to discredit collaborationists, to encourage and assist in the promotion of resistance and revolt against Axis control by the people of these territories, and to raise their morale and will to resist." The techniques authorized included "agent provocateurs, bribery, blackmail, rumors, forgery, false pamphlets, leaflets and graphics, and 'freedom stations' masquerading as the voice of groups resistant within enemy and enemy occupied countries when used for subversive deception."

MOSSAD LE ALIYAH BETH (MOSSAD)

The Israeli intelligence agency with responsibility for gathering and analyzing information abroad, and for taking active measures against foes of the Israeli state. Formally, "The Institution for Intelligence and Special Assignments." Given extraordinarily free rein by Israeli public opinion, Mossad's eye-for-an-eye retaliations against such enemies as the Palestine Liberation Organization make it a much-feared organization. Intelligence experts put Mossad at the top rank of the world's agencies, on a par with CIA and KGB.

Mossad is a lineal descendant of a cluster of intelligence and security forces that date to pre-independence days. The major ancestors are the *Shai,* the intelligence division of *Haganah,* the underground army created by Jewish settlers in Palestine; the *Shin Beth,* responsible for internal security; and *Aliyah Beth,* which helped homeless Jews get into the then-British mandate. The Foreign Ministry (after 1948) had its own intelligence section for liaison with allied agencies, and there was a police intelligence unit as well.

In 1951, Prime Minister Ben Gurion reorganized the sprawling structure. *Aliyah Beth* and police intelligence remained intact. Two other groups emerged. *Aman* took responsibility for military intelligence, in close alignment with the armed forces. The new agency, *Mossad,* took on the broad range of duties that its title, "special assignments," would suggest.

Mossad's central office is on Oliphant Street in the Talbieh section of Jerusalem.

MOTHERHOOD
See AGENT OF INFLUENCE.

MOTHER "K"
CIA jargon for Langley headquarters, derived from the cryptonym for its headquarters, KUBARK.

MOUCHARD
Double agent, in French.

MOVEMENTS ANALYSIS
Term for a constant surveillance of the daily travels of officials of a Soviet embassy and its satellite offices, such as other bloc embassies, trade missions, the Aeroflot airline, the TASS news agency, and the like. By close and prolonged study of these movements, counterintelligence agents pinpoint which officials do legitimate diplomatic business, and which seem to be engaged in spying. James Bennett, a counterespionage spe-

cialist for the Royal Canadian Mounted Police, developed movements analysis as a means of keeping tabs on Soviet diplomats in Ottawa. A variation of the system is now used by all other Western intelligence agencies. Movements analysis gave MI5 the evidence that was used as the justification for expelling 105 Soviets from Britain in 1971. MI5 had more than 300 persons on its list; only the most flagrant were thrown out of the country.

The Soviets now counter movements analysis by dispatching nonintelligence personnel on rounds that parallel those of actual agents—the aim being to occupy and confuse Western counterintelligence people.

MUGBOOK

A photographic album or file maintained in CIA stations that contains the picture and brief biographical sketch of hostile intelligence agents operating in the area. New agents are expected to spend hours studying the mugbook so that they can spot KGB or other unfriendly operatives at a glance. This knowledge is useful when an agent needs to know whether he is under surveillance. Friendly police and intelligence agencies help keep the mugbooks current by providing photographs of diplomatic personnel who go through customs control at international airports.

MUSIC BOX

A radio transmitter (KGB).

MUSICIAN

KGB term for a radio operator.

MYTHS ABOUT THE SPY TRADE

• That the FBI cut back on wiretaps temporarily each year before Director J. Edgar Hoover's appearance before the House Appropriations Committee. If asked about the number of bugs in operation, Hoover could give a deceptively low figure. Not so. The Church Committee found no significant blips in the number of taps before, during, or after Hoover's testimony during the five-year period. In 1970, for instance: on February 5, the Bureau maintained 39 wiretaps; when Hoover testified on March 5, there were 36 taps; on April 7, there were 37 taps.

• That Mata Hari never exposed her breasts while dancing (although she was liberal in affording audiences views of other anatomical regions) because her first husband, Randolph Mac-Leod, a British army officer, had bitten off her breasts in a jealous rage before leaving her. (He was suspicious of her from the outset, having made her acquaintance through a blind matrimonial ad.) In fact, Ms. Hari performed frequently in the buff, and the French autopsy report after her execution showed no such deformity.

• That Mata Hari was a woman of exotic Indian heritage who first danced in the nude at age twelve in a religious ceremony. Actually, she was born Margaretha Zelle, daughter of a Dutch shopkeeper. Her first husband, MacLeod, took her to India soon after they wed; whatever she knew of Indian customs came from that brief sojourn.

• That the British Secret Intelligence Service selects cover names for agents from the 1914 London telephone directory. "A chestnut of a story heard by every schoolboy in the United Kingdom, but not true at all," deposes a veteran of the SIS who once worked with such matters.

n

NASHI

Russian word for "ours," meaning in KGB slang an agent or collaborator. In an attempt to neutralize defectors and anti-Communist nationalists, the KGB tried in the 1950s and 1960s to spread the impression that anyone who spoke native Russian was *nashi*. The ploy did not succeed. *(See also* SVOI.)

NATIONAL ALLIANCE OF RUSSIAN SOLIDARITY (NTS)

An anti-Communist Russian exile group formed in Yugoslavia in post-czarist days. CIA took control of the willing NTS in the late 1940s and used its members for a host of espionage and line-crossing missions. Persons recruited from within NTS trained at a camp in Badwiesse, Upper Bavaria; and also at the U.S. Army's Intelligence School, Fort Holabird, Maryland; the Special Warfare School, Fort Bragg, North Carolina; and at CIA's Camp Peary near Williamsburg, Virginia.

NTS's goal was to proselytize liberal Russian exiles and to overthrow Communism in the USSR and replace it with a democratic parliamentary system. Leaders carefully screened members; they scorned the royalist philosophies of White Russians, and they would admit no person above thirty-five years of age. The German-born intelligence expert Louis Hagen (a British resident after 1936) compared its politics to the right wing of the British Labor Party, or to the left wings of the American Democratic and Republican parties.

NATIONAL INTELLIGENCE AUTHORITY (NIA)

An executive council created by President Truman on January 22, 1946, to exert authority over the simultaneously created

Central Intelligence Group (CIG). NIA was a predecessor to the National Security Council. Now defunct.

NATIONAL INTELLIGENCE DAILY

A Washington newspaper that has perhaps the most tightly controlled circulation (sixty copies)—and most authoritative information—of any in the world. Published by CIA, the *NID* presents Agency daily reports in newspaper format, with brief summaries at the head of each story for the hurried reader. William Colby instituted the format soon after becoming Director of Central Intelligence in 1974, to "emphasize the more important items and to offer the recipient the choice between a quick headline summary and reading in depth." (Colby first broached the newspaper idea while a junior officer in Stockholm in the early 1950s; the then-DCI, Allen Dulles, rejected the proposal. When Colby "suggested" the newspaper again, he was DCI. Publication began promptly.)

NATIONAL INTELLIGENCE ESTIMATE (NIE)

An estimate of the capabilities, vulnerabilities, and probable courses of action of foreign nations—friendly, enemy, and neutral. Although issued under the signature of the director of Central Intelligence, an NIE represents the composite view of the intelligence community. Individual agencies can express their dissent from consensus opinion through footnotes or addenda. In addition to national and regional studies, the intelligence community also produces periodical "Estimates of the World Situation." By custom, "Copy Number One" goes onto the desk of the President of the United States.

NATIONAL RECONNAISSANCE OFFICE (NRO)

The United States government agency responsible for managing satellite reconnaissance programs for the entire intelligence community. Although assigned to the United States Air Force for cover purposes (under the Under Secretary of the Air Force and the Office of Space Systems), NRO in fact is run by the National Reconnaissance Executive Committee, which is chaired by the director of Central Intelligence. President Eisenhower created NRO in 1960 as an outgrowth of the U-2 plane incident to give better management to the space and aerial reconnaissance program. NRO's existence was accidentally revealed to the public by a Senate committee in 1973, which listed it among the intelligence agencies that should make their budgets public. The Department of Defense annual report says only that NRO is charged with "the collection of specialized foreign intelligence through reconnaissance programs." NRO is located in Room 4C-956 of the Pentagon. It works closely with the three major developers of reconnaissance satellites: Hughes, TRW, and Lockheed. Officially, the government does not acknowledge the existence of NRO. Admiral Stansfield Turner, the former director of Central Intelligence, has complained to friends that CIA vetters forced him to use a euphemism when he mentioned NRO in his memoirs, published in 1985.

NATIONAL SECURITY AGENCY (NSA)

The agency responsible for the security of United States communications and for breaking the codes and ciphers used by other nations. President Truman created NSA by executive order on October 24, 1952; its predecessor was the Armed Forces Security Agency. NSA's existence was not officially acknowledged until 1957, although it occupies a conspicuously large building on the Fort Meade military reservation, easily visible from the Baltimore-Washington Parkway. NSA is arguably the most secretive agency in the American intelligence community.

NATIONAL SECURITY COUNCIL INTELLIGENCE DIRECTIVE (NSCID, or NEE-SID)

The formal order by which the National Security Council directs CIA or another intelligence agency to carry out an assigned mission. NSCIDs tend to be general, with the objective shrouded in euphemistic language. The nuts and bolts are defined more specifically in a follow-up paper called the "Director of Central Intelligence Directive," or DCID ("dee-cid").

The NSC (for a nonexistent example) might talk about the hostile attitude of the government of Jamaica and suggest "exploratory measures" to bring about a friendly successor. The DCID would go into the specifics of how to finance opposition parties, and the adverse propaganda that could persuade Jamaicans to change governments. Put side by side, no direct connection could be made between the NSCID and the DCID. Unless, of course, one understood the implications of the NSCID. *(See also* DIRECTOR OF CENTRAL INTELLIGENCE DIRECTIVE.)

NATIONAL VOICE OF IRAN (NVOI)

A clandestine radio station that has broadcast into Iran from Soviet Azerbaijan since 1959, representing itself as the voice of unidentified "progressive" elements of the Iranian people. NVOI's purpose is to promote Soviet policies in Iran, and to spread anti-U.S. propaganda. During the seizure of the U.S. embassy in 1979–80, NVOI praised the "struggling young people . . . [who] proved to the world the conspiracies and intrigues of U.S. officials against Iran." Formally, the Soviet government disavows any knowledge of or connection with NVOI. NVOI is a black propaganda operation, but one that does not deceive Western intelligence.

NAVAJO CODE TALKERS

Native American Navajo Indians who served as radio communicators with the Marine Corps during World War II. Battlefield conditions do not permit the use of ciphers, so the Marines were temporarily stymied in developing a secure means of radio talk. Phillip Johnston, an engineer and son of Navajo missionary parents, suggested Navajo radiomen, noting that their verbal forms and tonal characteristics would be totally incomprehensible to the Japanese. He was correct and the Navajo Code Talkers contributed mightily to the Marine victory at Guadalcanal.

NEIGHBOR

A KGB term for another Soviet intelligence agency operating in the same country, or the same embassy. Under the Soviet system, no single "chief" controls all intelligence operations in a country; the KGB has its own operations, as do the GRU, the trade ministry, and other agencies.

"NEVER BE A CAREY"

Irish imprecation against becoming an informer or traitor. The nineteenth-century informer James Carey told the British the identity of one-time comrades who assassinated many high officials in Ireland. *(See also* INFORMANT.)

NEVER SAY ANYTHING

Play on the initials of the ultra hush-hush National Security Agency, which, outsiders maintain, does not acknowledge even to itself the fact of its existence.

NINHYDRINE, NIN

A color reagent that is an internal security agent's favored friend. The reddish-black powder is lightly sprinkled on files where unauthorized hands are thought to be prowling. These hands almost immediately turn vivid violet when the ninhydrine—"nin," in spookspeak—reacts with the amino acid in the skin. Three days are required for the color to fade, and washing only makes it worse. Because it is easily visible to the eye, nin is useful for catching the village-idiot type of spy.

NKO

Need to know only, as in "This report should be distributed on an NKO basis."

NOFODIS

"No foreign dissemination"—a subcategory of classification that means a document must not be circulated outside the United States government. The nofodis designation can be used either to protect a particularly sensitive source of information or to conceal U.S. interest in an event elsewhere in the world.

NOISE

A mass of information that hindsight analysis proves to be useless or irrelevant, but that cannot be readily sorted through by the contemporary analyst or decision-maker. Roberta Wohl-stetter, who wrote the landmark study on Pearl Harbor *(Pearl Harbor: Warning and Decision),* coined the term, concluding that "we failed to anticipate [the attack] not for want of the relevant materials, but because of a plethora of irrelevant ones." The creation of diversionary noise is an intelligence agency's role in any sizable military operation—e.g., the deceptions employed before the June 1944 invasion of Europe during World War II.

NONDISCERNIBLE MICROBIOINOCULATOR

The tongue-twisting term that DCI William Colby used, to describe a dart gun for firing lethal toxins, in an appearance before the Church Committee. Although the gun was never used and Colby volunteered the fact of its existence, the Church Committee brandished it during public hearings as an example of the perfidious weapons in CIA's arsenal. Colby's embarrassment was alleviated by his special counsel, Mitchell Rogovin. When a committee staff member dropped the gun on a table in front of Colby, Rogovin hastily scooped it up and handed it to Senator Frank Church. Hence Colby was not photographed with the "nondiscernible microbioinoculator" in hand. Many persons in CIA, active and retired, felt Colby was grandstanding, showing off unused tradecraft to curry favor with the Committee.

NOT-TO-CONTACT LIST

An FBI file on reporters and newspapers that had been critical either of the bureau or of director J. Edgar Hoover. Persons or organizations on this list received a brushoff when they sought information from the bureau. The bureau ran name-checks (i.e., a review of its computerized files) on reporters before extending them any cooperation on a story. If anything in the reporter's personal or professional life was suspect, he would be ignored.

NOT WITTING

A person not cognizant of the existence of a classified project, although he might be involved in it as part of his normal course of business. Such a person can also be called "unwitting." (See also WITTING.)

NOTIONAL

A British coinage of World War II vintage has come to have diverse meanings. Originally, "notional" described the multi-

level deceptions the British used against the Germans, and referred, in particular, to the misinformation fed back to Berlin
after German agents had been captured and neutralized. The
aim was to give the Germans imaginary but credible information that would convince them their agent was energetically
active. For instance, according to Ewen Montague of the disinformation directorate, "a double agent notionally went to
Bristol and notionally saw a ship (which may or may not have
been there)." But the ship sighting was reported as gospel truth.

In current usage, notional has taken on expanded meaning. In
positive intelligence, notionals are fictitious, private commercial
companies that exist solely on paper, as the ostensible employer
of intelligence personnel, or as the ostensible sponsor of activities in support of clandestine operations. In this context, notional can be applied to many of the "proprietary" companies
the CIA has created to mask its covert activities.

To the FBI, however, a notional is a splinter group set up (by
the bureau itself) to draw away membership from a target organization, thereby disrupting or destroying it. During its
COINTELPRO project, the FBI ran three separate types of notional organizations:

• An organization whose members are all bureau informants.
In one scheme, the FBI created an all-informant branch of a
Communist group in a southern city. The initial purpose was to
cause the Communist Party USA the expense of sending organizers to the area to work with the ostensibly friendly club
and financing the travel of its members to national functions.
The ultimate goal of members was to begin to deviate from the
CPUSA line and be expelled from the main organization, so
they "could claim to be the victim of a Stalinist-type purge."

• A notional organization with some unsuspecting (non-in-
formant) members, intended to drain strength from the target
group. For instance, in one southern city the FBI set up a Klan
organization to attract members from the United Klans of
America and managed to grow to a strength of some 250 persons.

• A wholly fictitious organization, with no actual members,
used solely to mail letters or pamphlets attacking the target
group. To use another example from the FBI COINTELPRO
project, "The Committee for Expansion of Socialist Thought in
America" for years attacked the CPUSA from the position of

the "Marxist right." The "committee" consisted of one FBI agent, a letterhead, and a post office box mailing address.

Numerous CIA notionals, created to counter Communist organizations in Western Europe during the Cold War years, remain active and unrevealed. An informal rule of thumb is that CIA has its own counterpart to any front group that the Communists and their fellow-travelers manage to devise.

NOVATOR

KGB term, an acronym of the Russian words *novye*, for new, and *torit*, to flatten. It refers to a newly recruited agent abroad: a *novator* is newly flattened and owned by KGB.

N.R.A.

"*Nothing Recorded Against*." British term for findings of no adverse information when a person is subjected to a security investigation.

NUGGET

British term for bait to be offered a potential defector—a woman, money, political asylum, or a piece of information.

NUMBER CRUNCHERS

The massive computers used by the National Security Agency to break encrypted messages plucked from the sky by electronic intelligence sources.

NURSEMAID

KGB officers who accompany Soviet delegations or touring groups that travel abroad. They are alert for any evidence of errant behavior or dangerous associations with foreigners. If the nursemaid *(nyanki* in Russian) sees anything out of the ordinary, the suspect Russian is shipped home immediately. The *nyanki* takes no chances: if he permits a Soviet citizen to defect, he faces a sentence to a labor camp in Siberia or even, in rare cases, execution for treason.

O

OBSERVATION POST (OP)

An apartment or office that overlooks a target of intelligence interest, such as the rear of a Soviet embassy or the entrance to the Cuban Mission to the United Nations in New York. CIA regularly uses non-Agency employees ("grannies") to live in OPs and pays the bulk of the rent. In return, Agency technicians and photographers use the OP to take photographs of persons entering or leaving the target building and to monitor room microphones and sophisticated directional listening equipment. The grannies frequently are retired couples, hence the name.

OFFICE OF STRATEGIC SERVICES (OSS)

The United States' dominant intelligence agency during World War II. Formally created by President Roosevelt in June 1942 (after months of shadow existence), OSS gathered strategic and economic intelligence; conducted espionage, sabotage, and paramilitary operations; coordinated and supplied underground resistance movements; and made general mischief against the Axis. OSS was run by Major General William Donovan, a Medal of Honor winner in World War I, and a lawyer with a lifelong interest in intelligence matters—so much so, in fact, that the FBI's J. Edgar Hoover and the military intelligence establishment considered "Wild Bill" a sworn enemy. Hoover succeeded in keeping OSS out of South America, and General Douglas MacArthur would not permit it to operate in his Pacific Theater. But given a free hand elsewhere, OSS flourished. President Truman curtly abolished the agency on October 1, 1945, bowing to ill-defined fears that a "super-intelligence service" might arise in postwar America. OSS was reborn a few years later, in somewhat modified form, as the Central Intelligence Agency.

OFFSET ARRANGEMENTS

A system that prevents deep-cover CIA employees from becoming rich through their cover jobs. Any income earned from these jobs, or from cover businesses, is "offset" against the employee's CIA salary. Any money earned in excess of the salary eventually goes to the U.S. Treasury. The bottom line is that the officer receives only his government salary. (Also called "offset money.")

OH SO SOCIAL (OSS)

Derogatory term for the wartime Office of Strategic Services, based upon the fact that much of its hierarchy was drawn from graduates of Ivy League schools and socially proper New York law and brokerage firms. (Ironically, the OSS director, General Donovan, was the son of an Irish-American railroad worker, born in a waterfront district in Buffalo, New York, light years distant from the Social Register.) Derision aside, the "tea cup spies" were useful because much high-level political and economic intelligence could be gleaned from drawing room talks with princes and industrialists. At its zenith, OSS ranks contained such a medley of personnel—ranging from American academics to European emigré fighters to downright thugs and safecrackers—that the Oh So Social label was not taken seriously by anyone who knew the organization.

ONE-SHOT

An informant who thinks he can make a one-time deal with an intelligence agency, exchanging an item of singularly important information for a large amount of money. Such seldom happens. In the words of former CIA case officer William Hood, "Grasping greenhorns have about as much chance of swinging a deal like this as the average football fan would have of surviving more than a few minutes in a Super Bowl game."

ONE-TIME PAD

A code system that relies upon the sender and the receiver having identical copies of "pads," usually some 50 pages, each covered with lines of letters or figures chosen at random. The person sending the coded message uses letters or numbers from one of the pages; the receiver, who is told the page being used that day, consults his copy of the pad to decipher the message. Since each page is different, the code is unbreakable. The risk is that a field agent will have to discard his pads in an emergency, thereby losing his ability for clandestine communication with his control. The German Foreign Office initiated the use of one-time pads in the early 1920s. The Germans used pads of 50 numbered sheets, each legal-sized, containing 48 five-digit groups distributed in eight lines of six groups each. "Each 240 digits were random, and no sheet duplicated any other," writes code expert David Kahn. "For the first time in history, the official communications of a government were absolutely secure against the prying eyes of others." Oddly, although the fundamentals of the system were developed—and patented—by an American, Gilbert S. Vernam, the United States military did not adopt it until the eve of World War II.

ON THE GROUND

To place a new or prospective agent under light surveillance is to see what he or she looks like "on the ground." CIA routine procedure in the 1960s was to conduct a loose surveillance of any "walk-in" who volunteered information, to determine whether he was controlled by a rival agency. U.S. tradecraft is for such a recruit to break any contact with discernible intelligence agencies before making his overture to the opposition. The Soviets—through the 1960s, at least—were not as careful.

OPEN TEXT

Message sent in uncoded form. An intelligence agent operating in unfriendly territory routinely encodes the most innocuous of dispatches.

OPERATIONAL CLIMATE

The gist of the political, economic, and cultural situation in a given country that is the target of intelligence efforts—a situation that, for better or worse, facilitates intelligence activity in the country of the opponent. The most important (and obvious) requisites are one's freedom to stay anywhere in the country without reporting to the police, to select one's profession freely, and the absence of one's need to carry official identification and show it upon demand. Soviet-bloc intelligence services also list these other criteria for possible espionage:

• The strength, capability, professionalism, technical equipment, and effort expended by the opponent's intelligence and counterintelligence services;

• The attitude of the individual citizen toward his own country—patriotism, pride in being a citizen, and the willingness, in case of need, to lay down one's life;

• The patriotism of those individuals who are the principal targets of intelligence efforts—cultural, political, and economic circles;

• The coexistence of various ethnic groups of citizens and their ability to mutually tolerate each other or the disputes between them;

• The amount of crime in the country;

• The professionalism of the police apparatus, its technical equipment level, and the average rate of uncovered and punished crimes;

• The level of education of the average citizen and his general political outlook;

• The attitude of the average citizen toward intelligence and counterintelligence officers. (According to defector Josef Frolik, "The Czechoslovak Intelligence Service, along with the intelligence services of the other Communist countries, have a professional respect for the intelligence agencies of the United States. This point results in the fact that the overall agent environment [in the United States] is evaluated as being very negative with respect to the Communist intelligence services.")

Agent Environment is the Soviet bloc services' term for what CIA calls "operational climate."

OPERATIONAL INTELLIGENCE
In CIA usage, the information necessary to identify potential agents, their tastes, their attitudes, and people with access to them and through whom American intelligence could work. CIA's William Colby felt that operational intelligence often became "an end unto itself." Much energy was expended on learning inside information on Communist embassies and how

they worked internally, and in finding local citizens who had contacts with the Communist diplomats and who would find even more information. According to Colby, too often these persons proved to be in minor positions and to possess minor information. A contrary view, expressed by a CIA official with long experience in Western Europe, goes as follows: "Get your foot in the door, and keep it there, and eventually you'll come up with significant information." This official expresses what is known as the "Fuller Brush Man" approach to intelligence: "You gotta make housecalls to make sales, and you gotta make housecalls to get intelligence."

OPERATIONAL USE

Using a person, group, organization, or privileged information in a clandestine operation or in support of a clandestine activity.

OPERATIVE

See AGENT.

ORCHESTRA

In Abwehr (German military intelligence) usage during World War II, any espionage organization working against the Reich. Abwehr procedure was to subtitle "orchestras" according to their areas of operation ("Maritime Orchestra" or "Brussels Orchestra"). Hence when the Abwehr detected an "organization" reporting to Moscow, it became the famed *Rote Kappelle,* or "Red Orchestra," one of the more successful intelligence rings of World War II.

ORDER OF BATTLE (OB)

Information regarding the identity, strength, command structure, and disposition of personnel, units, and equipment of any military force. OB intelligence is usually compiled and maintained by the military services, which further breaks the information down into "Tables of Organization," or personnel strength, and "Tables of Equipment," or materiel. The OB enables a commander to know the strength and composition of forces facing him on the battlefield. Changes in the OB can indicate strategic decisions. For instance, intelligence officers in

General Douglas MacArthur's Far East Command in the spring of 1950 noticed that the North Korean People's Army (NKPA) was moving numerous tank units toward the 38th Parallel, the demarcation line between North and South Korea. MacArthur's intelligence chief, Major General Charles Willoughby, dismissed the OB shifts as insignificant. Several weeks later the tank units spearheaded the Communist invasion of South Korea. Five months later, MacArthur and Willoughby similarly ignored other OB intelligence suggesting Chinese Communist intervention in the Korean War. These two episodes support the axion: "Intelligence is only as good as the people using it."

ORGANIZATIONAL COVER

The use of legitimate corporation offices abroad (as well as non-intelligence U.S. government agencies) as a cover for covert agents. The preferred procedure is for CIA to obtain the blessing of a senior corporate executive, although on occasion no one in the company will be witting of his true mission. Working under organizational cover is onerous because the agent usually must perform his corporate job for credibility purposes; thus only his evenings and weekends (and other odd moments) can be given to CIA. Further, his corporate salary goes into the U.S. Treasury, and he must live on his agency income (although he might draw extra expenses if his corporate job requires a high lifestyle).

The corporations that provide cover to CIA vary from year to year; obvious ones would be airlines, banks, and trading companies. Of the myriad U.S. agencies, only one is strictly off limits to CIA cover assignments: the Peace Corps. *(See also* COVER ORGANIZATIONS.*)*

OUTSIDE MAN

A CIA case officer who works abroad as an ostensible private citizen with no overt contacts with either the CIA station or the United States Embassy. *(See also* DEEP COVER; INSIDE MAN.*)*

p

P.4
A super-secret branch of MI6, the British intelligence service, which "persuades" professionals such as attorneys, physicians, and accountants to pass along information concerning national security that they obtain from clients. P.4's very existence violates ethical standards of the relevant professional societies; thus it is an unacknowledged activity. CIA briefly considered such a section in the late 1950s, but rejected it on ethical grounds. The British felt no such constraint.

PACKED UP
Phrase describing an intelligence operation that is terminated, either because of failure or fear of exposure.

PANEL SOURCES
FBI informants who are not involved in a group under investigation, but who will "attend its public gatherings on behalf of [the] FBI for intelligence purposes or as potential witnesses." Panel sources were first developed to act as witnesses in Smith Act trials of Communist Party members in the 1950s, when it was necessary to prove such simple facts as the existence of the CPUSA, the dates and places of public meetings held by the party, and similar matters. To avoid surfacing regular informants within the CPUSA to establish such facts, the FBI developed panel sources. Some of these panel sources were pressed into service involuntarily. During the 1960s, one of my reportorial colleagues was directed to attend a Communist meeting; when he returned, he was instructed to write not a news story, but a "memo for the FBI," summarizing what had happened. He protested—"I'm a newspaperman, not a spy"—but complied. Later the reporter was called to testify at a deportation

proceeding involving one of the persons who had spoken at the meeting.

PAPAKHA

Russian word for "big hat," used by KGB underlings to denote officials of importance in their organization. The less-liked *papakhas* are called *zhopas* (literally, asses). A CIA recruiter who hears a target call his superior a *zhopa* knows that he is fishing in promising waters.

PAPER MERCHANT

An unscrupulous person who manufactures "intelligence reports" out of whole cloth and peddles them to one or more services. Such con men thrived in Western Europe in the late 1940s and early 1950s, to the acute embarrassment of both Western and Soviet bloc agencies. Many sold the same bogus reports both to CIA and MI6. Given agencies' zealousness in protecting covert sources, such subterfuges could go undetected for months, with the similar reports (although coming from the same source) confirming one another.

One paper merchant who achieved singular success in World War II turned to fraud when he found purity of motive was not sufficient qualification for joining British intelligence. Felipe Fernandez, a left-wing Spanish journalist, volunteered his services to SIS in 1941 but was rejected because of Communist leanings. Undeterred, Fernandez sought out the Abwehr. The Germans hired Fernandez, and he took up quarters in Lisbon and flooded the Abwehr with elaborate reports, supposedly coming from a vast network he controlled in England. ARABEL (as the Abwehr called Fernandez) had as his only tools a fertile imagination and a guidebook to Britain. But the Germans bought his reports, whereupon he returned to SIS, documented his contacts, and was taken in as double agent GARBO. Through May 1945, when the European war ended, GARBO/ ARABEL supplied the Germans with literally hundreds of bogus reports, receiving in return 20,000 pounds. The Germans gave Fernandez the Iron Cross; the British, the King's Medal for Service in the Cause of Freedom.

PARAMILITARY FORCES, PARAS

Units of soldiers not attached to the formal military services of any nation, even though they might resemble conventional armed forces in organization, equipment, training, or mission. Paras range from small training missions that work with local friendly soldiers to vast organizations such as the brigade of Cuban exiles that comprised the Bay of Pigs invasion force. CIA has traditionally served as the cover organization for American paramilitary forces, members of which are drawn from the armed service, mercenaries, and local armies. An American assigned to paramilitary duty with CIA "resigns" from his service, with the understanding that he can reenter without loss of rank or seniority upon completion of the mission.

During the 1960s and 1970s, CIA relied heavily upon foreign recruiting of so-called soldiers of fortune to support friendly governments and oppose Communist takeovers of emerging African nations. (So, too, did former colonial powers such as Belgium and France, which tried to maintain toeholds in their former holdings.) Contrary to popular legend, CIA recruited through intermediaries, and *not* through the classified advertisements of such adventure magazines as *Soldier of Fortune.*

Another source of paras is soldiers caught on the losing side of a revolution or coup. For instance, CIA more or less openly supported Nicaraguan exiles opposing the leftist Sandinista government that took power in that Central American nation in the late 1970s. Working from bases on the Nicaraguan border, these paras conducted enough sabotage and espionage missions to keep the government on edge (CIA's intention being to dissuade the Sandinistas from military adventure and subversion elsewhere in Central America).

The free-booting life of a para is offset by the fact that, since he belongs to no organized military force and wears no recognized uniform, he is subject to being shot as a spy if captured.

PASSWORD
See RECOGNITION SIGNAL.

PATRICE LUMUMBA UNIVERSITY

A KGB-conducted school in Moscow for Third World youths, many of whom arrive in the USSR expecting to be trained as physicians, but instead are schooled in sabotage, bomb-making, and other terrorist tactics. The youths are kept segregated from the general Soviet population, to avoid undue exposure to the anti-black racism endemic in the USSR.

PENETRATION

The process by which an intelligence agent gains access to the organization and work of another intelligence service, unknown to the latter.

PERSONA NON GRATA-ed (PNG-ed)

The diplomatic term for a person who is told to leave the host country because of unacceptable conduct. Since many spies operate under diplomatic cover and hence have immunity from arrest, they are "persona non grata-ed" when caught. (The verb form of the word, which might cause grief to a philologist, is nonetheless common among both diplomats and spooks.)

Many such cases never reach public view because the host country chooses not to make a major issue of the offense. One such instance was a Czech intelligence plot in 1958 to have an agent put atropine salt into shakers in a cafeteria of Radio Free Europe in Salzburg, Austria. (RFE is a major target of the Soviet and bloc intelligence services.) Atropine can cause hallucinations and, in great enough quantities, even death. But the person given the assignment was a double who worked concurrently for CIA and exposed the plot. The Czech intelligence official responsible, Jaroslav Nemec, who had diplomatic immunity as a "vice consul," was PNG-ed out of the country—quickly but quietly.

Ph.D. INTELLIGENCE

A term of derision J. Edgar Hoover, the late director of the FBI, used to describe the archrival Central Intelligence Agency. Hoover so detested the CIA and its "Ivy League" director, Richard Helms, that he severed all liaison with the Agency during his latter years.

PIG

KGB term for a traitor.

PIGEON

The target of a surveillance.

PIGGYBACKING

Relying upon a friendly intelligence agency to supply the fruits of a covert investigatory technique, such as the result of a wiretap or a bug. For years Western intelligence agencies piggybacked on one another throughout the world—the British providing information from its former protectorates in the Arab nations; the Americans watching Latin America and parts of Western Europe; the Israelis spying on extremist Middle East nations. The exchange meant maximum coverage at minimal expense. Unfortunately, CIA's troubles of the mid-1970s caused several Western agencies, notably Israel's Mossad, to begin withholding previously shared information. Piggybacking has revived, to a large extent, since 1981.

PINKERTON

Agent of the Pinkerton Detective Agency, which served as the primary military intelligence arm of the U.S. Army during the Civil War and continued a close alliance with federal and local law enforcement agencies thereafter. During the late 1800s, the Pinkerton Agency performed many of the functions now under the purview of the FBI. In the 1900s, Pinkertons became notorious as strikebreakers who beat up pickets and wrecked union halls. The name remains a dirty one in labor circles.

PISCINE, La.

See SDECE.

PIT, THE

A basement area in CIA headquarters where classified documents are shredded, pulped, or burned (or combinations thereof). Through the 1970s, the residue was dumped into the Potomac, which flows a few hundred yards north of the building. Environmentalists complained of the pollution, so now CIA's destroyed secret papers are sold for landfill in West Virginia.

A secondary usage for "The Pit" refers to the round-the-clock operations centers that CIA divisions maintain to handle crisis situations. Because of the architectural style of the CIA building, these centers tend to be windowless rooms whose frenetic human activity overwhelms the capacity of the air-conditioning system.

PITCH
An attempt by an intelligence agency to recruit a person from the opposition.

PLANT
1. A listening or observation post used to provide a vantage point for watching a surveillance subject. An ongoing routine for an FBI field office is to establish "friendly relations" with the management of major hotels. Thus, if a surveillance subject suddenly rents a room and the bureau desires an adjoining room to use as a plant, any previous guest is quickly transferred elsewhere.

2. A person put into proximity to an investigative subject with the intention of exploiting a known or perceived weakness. When the FBI was trying to discredit the Rev. Martin Luther King, Jr., as a philanderer, for instance, an agent suggested "placing a good-looking female plant" in his office. Bearded about such a technique before the Church Committee, former FBI official William Sullivan called it a "common practice among intelligence services all over the world. This is not an isolated phenomenon. This is a common practice—tough, dirty business. Whether we should be in it or not, that is for you folks [the Senators] to decide. We are in it. . . . No holds were barred. We have used that technique against Soviet agents. They have used it against us." Sullivan, however, offered no defense for the campaign against Dr. King.

PLAYBACK
The reprinting, in another country, of false information that an intelligence agency managed to have published abroad. "Playback" is intended to give credibility to propaganda or disinformation campaigns. For instance, KGB will plant, in an Indian newspaper, a bogus story about American nuclear planning. When the story is picked up in Western Europe, it is

attributed to "the authoritative Indian political daily *Southern Hindustani Bugle.*" (Also known as *blowback* or *domestic fallout.*)

PLAY MATERIAL

Accurate information deliberately given a rival intelligence agency as a means of establishing the credibility of an agent who is attempting an infiltration. Since play material often involves turning one's own operative over to the enemy, it is an especially ruthless technique. In the 1950s, for instance, the KGB wished to infiltrate an agent named Nikita Khorunzki into the CIA-run National Alliance of Russian Solidarity (NTS), which was running missions into the Soviet Union. Khorunzki sought out a known CIA agent and told him that a somewhat overblown blonde with gold teeth was, simultaneously, the girlfriend of a lieutenant in the Soviet Army Mission in Frankfurt and a Soviet army deserter named Vassily Graburov. Checking his index, the CIA man discovered that Graburov had offered himself to American intelligence as an informer on KGB affairs. Surveillance quickly revealed that he was using the frowzy blonde as a courier to maintain contact with the Soviet lieutenant. Graburov was exposed and arrested. His bona fides now established, Khorunzki managed to secure a job as a teacher at the NTS espionage school at 53 Kaiser Friedrick Promenade in Bad Homburg. He stayed there—at unrevealed cost to NTS and CIA—for several years before being found out and sent to jail for fourteen years. Trial testimony suggested that he revealed details of specific NTS missions, as well as giving to KGB the names of NTS family members still in the Soviet Union.

PLUMBING

The support structure that enables agents to operate in the field. "Plumbing" is an all-inclusive term that means agents have detailed maps and train and subway schedules, as well as safe houses, clandestine letter-drops, surveillance teams, and technicians who can bug houses or apartments, tap phones, do clandestine photography, and find a bottle of Scotch at four in the morning. Generally the plumbers in this infrastructure are unaware of their ultimate employer. When an agency is preparing for an operation, the preliminary logistics are called "putting in the plumbing."

PNUTS ("Peanuts")

*P*ossible *N*uclear *T*est *S*ite. A word heard among U.S. Air Force intelligence officers.

POSITIVE VETTING

British security procedure wherein persons with access to classified material must be questioned and their background and previous associations and activities investigated and verified. Despite repeated security scandals, the British did not institute such a system until the mid-1950s. The American version, the "background investigation," or "full-field investigation," dates to the early days of World War II.

PRELIMINARY INVESTIGATION

A first-phase FBI probe of a subject whose involvement in criminal, subversive, or extremist activities is questionable or unclear. It is undertaken to further define his involvement and to determine whether a statutory basis exists for a full investigation. According to the FBI Manual, a preliminary investigation is supposed to be confined to a review of public source documents, record checks, and "established sources" and informants. *(See also* ESTABLISHED SOURCE.)

PRETEXT INTERVIEW

A conversation in which the agent arranges to talk about one subject when he is really interested in a totally different matter. The relevant questions are casually interjected into the interview. A pretext interview can also be arranged for the sole purpose of gaining access to a house or office for an agent, who will then try to conceal a microphone or other listening device on the premises. *(See also* ELICITATION.)

PROBABLE ENEMY

See MAIN ENEMY.

PROBE MICROPHONE

A microphone that can be put into a wall and transmit conversations in the adjoining room. The installers must drill a hole to within a hair's-breadth of breaking the internal surface. In some FBI field offices, such a device is known as a "spike mike."

PROCESSING THE TAKE

Transcribing, translating, and analyzing the material gathered through telephone taps and room bugs. Processing scores of hours of such material is costly and difficult. Since the targets often have reason to suspect their conversations are being monitored, the material is considered "low-grade ore."

PROGRESSIVE JOURNALIST

See RABCOR.

PROPAGANDA

By OSS definition, the "deliberate direction or manipulation of information to secure a definite object. It is promotion masked as to its (1) origin or source; (2) interests involved; (3) methods employed; (4) intent; (5) content spread; and (6) results accrued to the target. . . . The contents of propaganda may range from absolute truth, through selection, distortion, half-truths to complete falsehood—what is appropriate in order to secure positive action."

PROPRIETARY COMPANY

An ostensibly private business firm or office created and operated by an intelligence agency, as a means of providing cover for secret operations. CIA runs two types of these companies. The "operating proprietaries" actually do business as private firms. They are incorporated where they are officed, they file the applicable state and federal tax returns, and they obtain the licenses necessary to a legitimate business operation. (They also have been known to earn substantial profits.)

There is also the "nonoperating proprietary," sometimes called a "notional." Consisting of a letterhead, a mailing address, and a phone number, this type is essentially a mail-drop business based in the office of a friendly (although non-CIA) law or business firm. The "notional" aspect gives a covert agent a visible means of support; for instance, if he claims to work for Sunshine Enterprises, Ltd., in Washington, such a company can be found in the phone book, and someone will answer the telephone when it rings, and respond to mail.

In at least two instances, CIA used proprietaries for operations that skirted violating the law prohibiting Agency domestic operations. One such proprietary was an ostensibly private security company in the Washington, D.C., metropolitan area, which was controlled by CIA's Office of Security and was used for operations where no government identification was permissible, or where other considerations required "deep cover." In 1967, the Office of Security used the firm to monitor anti-war and other dissident groups for evidence of any actions planned against CIA facilities. Targeted were the Women's Strike for Peace, the Washington Peace Center, the Congress on Racial Equality, and the Student Nonviolent Coordinating Committee. The surveillance was low-level and amateurish, with the proprietary company hiring construction workers, other blue-collars, and members of their families. These "agents" received no deep training, and their reports to CIA were mostly useless. But the program continued until 1970, under the code name MERRIMAC. CIA justified MERRIMAC as an exercise of its statutory right to protect its physical facilities.

Another borderline proprietary dealt with telegraphic intercepts. Inundated with scores of thousands of cables recorded on a new magnetic tape system, the National Security Agency in 1966 pleaded with CIA for administrative help. Due to the dubious legality of its SHAMROCK interception program—whereby NSA snatched up 150,000 international telegrams monthly—NSA wished the messages to be processed discreetly. CIA obliged by renting office space in lower Manhattan under the guise of a television tape processing company, designated LPMEDLEY. For the next seven years, NSA read purloined cables in comfort and privacy, thanks to the CIA proprietary company. The Church Committee strongly criticized both MERRIMAC and LPMEDLEY. *(See also* NOTIONAL.)

PROTECTED INFORMATION

Information derived from clandestine sources. The fact that such information is known must often be concealed in order to protect the source.

PROTECTIVE SECURITY

British term that encompasses all measures taken to keep classified information out of unfriendly hands. Sir Martin Furnival Jones, while director of MI5, stated the formal definition in these sentences:

"The body of regulations which regulate the behaviour, in relation to security information, of those who have access to it and . . . the selection of those who have access to it. It involves the processes of selection which are supposed to weed out those who may be unreliable and it embraces also their supervision once they have been taken on. It involves their education in security, in the things they should do and the things they should not do when they have charge of security information. It embraces an enormous range of rules for the handling of classified material. . . . It embraces the physical measures taken for the protection of information, such as locks and safes, guards on buildings and pass systems. . . . In support of counter-espionage the Director of the Protective Security Branch is very much concerned with it."

PROVAL

"Calamity," in Russian; in KGB circles, an operation that has gone horribly awry, with much embarrassment to all parties involved. In CIA, a person held responsible for such a disaster is retired (as happened to principal figures in the Bay of Pigs); in KGB, the culprit is either shot or transported to Siberia. Historically, the Soviets seem less concerned about *provals* than do Western agencies, chiefly because they have the advantage of a closed society in which neither press nor politicians discuss failures, much less criticize them. *(See also* FLAP POTENTIAL.*)*

The worse *provals* in Soviet intelligence history occurred in the course of forty days in 1927: a police raid on the Soviet consulate in Peking, on April 6, which revealed incontrovertible evidence of spying; arrests in France four days later of numerous French Communists who admitted espionage; and finally, the breaking of a Soviet spy ring in London on May 12 that resulted in Britain severing diplomatic relations with the USSR. These *provals* were costly because the USSR at the time was trying to establish respectability in the world community.

PROVING IT OUT
Double-checking an agent's claimed veracity by attempting to verify easily provable portions of his reports. Haphazard, but a good method of catching an unimaginative cheat. For instance, if the agent claims to have obtained X information from Ambassador Y at an embassy reception, the control asks what Y was wearing, and what time the party broke up. The asking of the questions hints that the control knows what transpired at the party (and in fact he often does know). Fumbling answers suggest a liar, not an agent, is at work.

PROVOCATION
Having an agent propose or agree to a nefarious deed on behalf of an opposition intelligence agency. Once the opposition agrees, the offensive agency has "moral justification" to proceed with its own dirty deeds. In 1963, for instance, CIA had numerous meetings with a high Cuban official, code-named AMLASH, to discuss the assassination of Premier Fidel Castro. (AMLASH wanted a rifle with telescope; the CIA contact man gave him a fountain pen with a needle point and suggested he fill it with Black Leaf-40, a commercial poison.) There was much suspicion in CIA that Castro knew of CIA plots to kill him and that AMLASH talked with CIA as part of a provocation scheme. By macabre irony, CIA official Desmond Fitzgerald and AMLASH had their last meeting on November 22, 1963. When Fitzgerald left the meeting, he learned of President Kennedy's murder. The juxtaposition of the AMLASH plot and the JFK killing suggested that Castro ordered Kennedy murdered as a retaliation—a suspicion that is unlikely ever to be proved or disproved. The Church Committee spent months pursuing the theory with no success. (See also AGENT PROVOCATEUR.)

PROVOCATION AGENT
An agent whose sole function is to provide false information for ulterior purposes. His story might be palpably false; nonetheless, it sows suspicion wherever received and must be either confirmed or disproved. KGB has been known to try to mask serious intelligence operations by "flooding" the West with provocation agents, each of whom carries bizarre stories that

must be checked. KGB's hope is that Western counterintelligence will be so overworked that serious agents can slip
through the security nets.

PUTTING IN THE PLUMBING

Organizing the operational support facilities that are needed
before any significant intelligence operation is set into motion
—including safe houses, training facilities, covert paymasters,
even office staff and typewriters.

q

QUIET FLAP
See FLAP POTENTIAL.

QUIET ONES
Homosexuals used by the KGB for entrapment of Westerners or other targets. Quiet ones can be either male or female. The Soviet Union treats homosexuals harshly; hence for them KGB missions are a means of survival, even if only temporary.

r

RABBLE ROUSER INDEX

FBI file used to target persons for its CONINTELPRO operation. As field agents were instructed by FBI headquarters, "The Index will consist of the names, identifying data, and background information of individuals who are known rabble rousers and who have demonstrated by their actions and their speeches that they have a propensity for fomenting racial disorder. It is desired that only individuals of prominence who are of national interest be included in this index. Particular consideration should be given to . . . those individuals in this category who travel extensively. . . . The fact that an individual is on the Security Index or Reserve Index does not preclude his inclusion on the Rabble Rouser Index."

This guideline was issued in October 1967; a month later a further directive broadened coverage to include persons with a "propensity for fomenting" disorders affecting the "internal security," not just racial matters. Eventually the Rabble Rouser Index grew to cover a range of organizations from the Southern Christian Leadership Conference to the Black Panther Party, Ku Klux Klan, and Students for a Democratic Society.

RABCOR

Russian-language abbreviation for "worker-correspondent," a system of volunteer journalists that emerged during the first years of the Soviet regime. The *rabcors* were intended to replace the old "pro-capitalist, reactionary" journalists of the Czarist era; they were to write "progressive reports" on the status of Soviet society for *Pravda* and other party newspapers. In practice, the *rabcors* numbered more than three million and were a key element in the informer system that kept Soviet society subservient to Stalin. Little of what they wrote went into public print; their "stories" in fact were raw intelligence reports. So successful was the *rabcor* system that Soviet intelligence extended it to Western targets, with the emphasis on persons working in such strategic installations as military bases and telegraph offices. As has ben noted by David J. Dallin, "The great advantage of the *rabcors* as a cover for espionage was their appearance of legality; there could be no objection to a worker writing to his newspaper about happenings in an industrial plant. Even a *rabcor* who broke the rule of secrecy and sent reports from a military establishment could honestly deny any link to foreign intelligence." In many instances the *rabcors* seemed honestly ignorant of their true mission.

According to the *Small Soviet Encyclopedia* (quoted by Dallin), The *Daily Worker* in New York claimed 800 *rabcors* in 1934; the British *Daily Worker,* 600. *L'Humanité,* the French Communist journal, had 1,200 *rabcors* in 1928 and 4,000 in 1934. The Soviets placed so much emphasis on the *rabcors* that Maria Ulianova, Lenin's sister, was designated chief spokesman for the movement, and published a book in 1928 entitled *The Rabcor Movement Abroad.*

The term *rabcor* has long disappeared from the Western intelligence vocabulary. The *rabcors* survive under the name "progressive journalists."

The existence of the *rabcor* network—and the true nature of the "correspondents'" work—came to light during a French intelligence investigation in 1932. By turning a key French Communist overseer of *rabcor,* French agents revealed the extent of the espionage, and two Soviet agents directing the work were sent to prison. The court decried the fact that "French citizens and Communist militants . . . permitted themselves to be dragged into it by criminal propaganda of foreign origin."

RACKET, THE
The term intelligence professionals use in referring to their line of work; CIA term, circa the 1950s.

RADIO SECURITY SERVICE (R.S.S.)
A World War II arm of MI5 responsible for detecting, monitoring, and locating clandestine transmitters. R.S.S. had offices on Hanslope Park in Buckinghamshire, about 35 miles from

Oxford. Listening posts were scattered around Great Britain at strategic points; R.S.S. also benefited from some 1,500 amateur radio operators (called "Voluntary Interceptors") who worked from their homes. Transmissions of interest had to be transcribed by hand, as R.S.S. did not have sufficient recorders to give to each of the stations.

RATISSAGE

In German, literally, a rat hunt; World War II jargon for a counterespionage manhunt.

RAVEN

A male KGB spy. Ravens are chosen not for physical good looks, but for their ability to appeal to middle-aged women of influence who have learned not to expect the best—only attention and physical satisfaction.

The oft-repeated procedure is for the raven to make a casual contact with the target—at a cocktail party, at a museum, even on the street—and commence a low-key nonsexual approach. After the ultimate bedding comes the ultimate request for a "bit of help" on a newspaper article or other research. Hope and shame do the rest.

RAZVEDKA

The Russian word that translates literally as "true intelligence," defined by defected NKVD officer Alexander Orlov as that "procured by undercover agents and secret informants in defiance of the laws of a foreign country in which they operate."

READY FOR THE HIGH JUMP

KGB slang for an officer who fears that he is subject to assassination or dismissal from the service because of incompetence or internal political problems. An officer who deduces that he is "ready for the jump"—often signaled by an unexpected call for his return to Moscow—is apt to call the local CIA station and offer his services to the West.

RECOGNITION SIGNAL

A discreet but visible means of informing an unknown person—a control agent or cut-out—that you are the agent with whom he should make contact. For casual meets, the signal can be as innocuous as a specified magazine spread out on a bar or coffee table. The more important the mission, the higher the degree of sophistication, with the requirement of signal and countersignal, response and counterresponse. (By omitting the response, an apprehended agent can alert the contact that something has gone wrong.)

In the autumn of 1945, Alan Nunn May, a British scientist who had worked on nuclear projects in Canada, was ready to return to Britain to continue his research—and his spying for the Soviet Union. May, given the code name "Alek," received specific instructions on how to contact his new control agent:

1. Place.

   In front of the British Museum of London, on Great Russell Street, at the opposite side of the street, about Museum Street, from the side of Tottenham Court Road . . . Alek [May] walks from Tottenham Court Road, the contact man from the opposite side—Southampton Road.

2. Time.

   . . . [I]t should be more expedient to carry out the meeting at 20 o'clock [8 P.M.], if it should be convenient to Alek, as at 23 o'clock, it is too dark. In case the meeting should not take place in October, the time and day will be repeated in the following months.

3. Identification signs.

   Alek will have under his left arm the newspaper *Times,* the contact man will have in his left hand the magazine *Picture Post.*

4. The password.

   The contact man: "What is the shortest way to the Strand?"

   Alek: "Well, come along, I am going that way."

   In the beginning of the business conversation, Alek says, "Best regards from Mikel."

The sentencing justice decried May's "crass conceit [and] wickedness" in surrendering an important national secret and sent him to prison for ten years. (May, an ideological spy, sold out his adopted country for $700 cash and two bottles of whiskey.)

Recognition signals also can be bizarre. When atomic spy Klaus Fuchs met a Soviet contact in New York in 1944, he was to stand on a street corner with a tennis ball in his left hand. His contact would be wearing gloves and carrying a book with green binding and another pair of gloves. When he went to London the next year, Fuchs was instructed to stand outside the Mornington Crescent underground station the first Saturday of each month, holding five books bound with string and supported by two fingers; in his other hand he was to hold two additional books.

The Soviets traditionally used such elaborate signals, as witness the instructions given KGB agent Alexander Foote when he was to meet a contact in Geneva:

> I was to be wearing a white scarf and to be holding in my right hand a leather belt. As the clock struck noon, I would be approached by a woman carrying a string shopping bag containing a green parcel, and holding an orange in her hand.
>
> One would have thought that this would have been sufficient to enable anyone to contact anyone, even an unknown, in the middle of a Swiss street. The woman would ask me, in English, where I had bought the belt; and I was to reply that I had bought it in an ironmonger's shop in Paris. Then I was to ask her where I could buy an orange like hers, and she was to say that I could have hers for an English penny.
>
> Hardly sparkling dialogue, but sufficient to ensure that the meeting was foolproof and an example of the usual thoroughness of my employers.

The verbal part of the recognition signal is known to the KGB as a *parol*, a pair or two pairs of sentences that must be recited in precise prearranged sequence. When circumstances are such that an agent cannot comfortably carry around tennis balls or an orange—an embassy party, say, or a meeting in a business office—the KGB procedure is to use a verbal signal.

When the Swedish Colonel Stig Wennerstrom went to Washington as a Soviet spy in 1952, he carried a carefully arranged password. Someone from the Soviet embassy would say to him (in the course of normal diplomatic contact): "Nikolai Vasilovich asked to be remembered to you."

Wennerstrom was to reply: "Yes, I know him very well. We used to meet sometimes at Spiridonovka."

Wennerstrom heard the exchange from the Soviet air attaché during a protocol meeting. The men were alone, and the Swede started discussing business, only to have the other man clasp a hand over his mouth and gesture wildly toward the ceiling. "No, no," the Russian's warning stare mimed, "The walls have ears."

REFERENTURA

A specially secured room in a Soviet or Soviet-bloc embassy for meetings of members of the *rezidentura* (see below) and for safekeeping files and other support materials. According to Josef Frolik, a Czech intelligence officer who defected in 1969, the *referentura* is kept secure by the embassy's "internal group," which also does the nuts-and-bolts clerical and logistical work necessary to any bureaucracy.

RESISTANCE GROUP

OSS definition: "Individuals associated together in enemy-held territory to oppose the enemy by any and all means short of military operations, e.g., by sabotage, non-cooperation, etc." *(See also* GUERRILLAS.)

RENT-A-COPS

See SSD.

RETRACING THE ANALYSIS

A process of evaluating how an intelligence estimate went wrong. "The purpose is to discover who made what wrong assessments, based on what misleading information, from what sources now considered to be unreliable . . ." William Safire of *The New York Times* used this language in November 1984 in suggesting that CIA find out how it managed to miss Bulgarian involvement in the plot to murder Pope John Paul II.

REZIDENT, ILLEGAL

A Soviet agent, living abroad without official cover, usually with an assumed identity, who is responsible for controlling subordinate illegal agents working in his area. The illegal *rezident* has no contact with the Soviet embassy or any of its personnel, and he maintains his own communications with KGB Center. In terms of authority, the illegal *rezident* has the rank of the formal KGB *rezident*. But, if arrested, he cannot plead diplomatic immunity: he goes to jail. The most important illegal *rezident* ever bagged by the FBI—insofar as has been publicly disclosed, in any event—was Colonel Rudolph Abel of the KGB, apprehended in 1957.

REZIDENTURA

The KGB section of a Soviet embassy, the ranking officer of which is the *rezident,* who operates under diplomatic cover. The *rezident* is the equivalent of a CIA chief of station. Because a *rezident* must have senior status in KGB, his identity as an agent is usually known to Western agencies, and hence he does little actual spying while abroad. Some *rezidents* do roam the cocktail circuit, for hard drinking seems a prevalent trait. In Washington, the identity of the *rezident* is protected by a peculiar professional courtesy of the American press. Soon after the *Washington Post* ran stories in the late 1970s naming several CIA station chiefs, I suggested to a reporter there that he do an article about the then-KGB *rezident*. I even offered him a photograph of the *rezident* at play at a reception. "That isn't news," the *Post*'s man stated.

In the larger embassies—Washington, Bonn, London, and Paris—the GRU (Soviet military intelligence) often runs a *rezidentura* separate from that of KGB. GRU's sphere of interest covers both strategic and tactical intelligence, and seldom does the work overlap. A Soviet agent concerned with collecting strategic information goes where the trail takes him, with little regard to bureaucratic boundaries. Agents and analysts assigned to a strategic *rezidentura* tend to be the best and brightest the Soviets have to offer. But persons in a tactical branch of a *rezidentura* are generally restricted to operations within the country to which they are assigned.

RIDING SHOTGUN .

Sending a second agent to surveil (and safeguard) an intelligence officer who is to meet a contact under dangerous circumstances. The "first shotgun" is often deliberately visible, a sort of night-watchman deterrent. The "second shotgun," however, is prepared to do whatever is necessary to protect the agent.

RINGING THE GONG

The prediction, by a CIA station, of a revolution in the host country.

ROLLING UP A NET

Arresting members of an intelligence apparatus (net) after the initial detection of its existence.

ROOF

The role played by a KGB agent abroad in a covert capacity. In KGB jargon, the "legend" is the false biography given an agent by Moscow Center; the "roof" is the role that the agent assumes openly when he is sent to a new place. *(See also* LEGEND.*)*

RUMOR

A false but plausible story put into circulation with the aim of causing harm to one's adversary. A rumor is a technique of Morale Operations, but only as a secondary weapon. As stated by an OSS manual, "Rarely can they [rumors] by themselves change basic attitudes. Their function is to confirm suspicions and beliefs already latent; to give sense and direction to fears, resentments or hopes that have been built up by more materialistic causes; to tip the balance when public opinion is in a precarious state." The OSS, with its cupboard of psychologists and Madison Avenue admen turned operatives, created a recipe entitled "Properties of a Good Rumor":

> A good rumor is one which will spread widely in a form close to that of the original story. Probably the main factor determining whether it catches on is the degree to which it is adapted for the state of mind of the audience. In addition, successful rumors embody most of the following qualities:

(1) *Plausibility.* A plausible rumor is tied to *some* known facts, yet is incapable of total verification. It may exaggerate, but it stops short of the incredible. It frequently appears as an "inside" story.

(2) *Simplicity.* A good rumor uses only one central idea as a core. Its basic message is simple and thus easy to remember.

(3) *Suitability to task.* To summarize opinions or attitudes which are already widely accepted, slogan-type rumors are best. ("England will fight to the last Frenchman.") To introduce "information" which will help build up *new* attitudes, however, narrative-type rumors are best (e.g., rumors which "prove" that Hitler is mentally ill).

(4) *Vividness.* Regardless of length or type, rumors which stimulate clear-cut mental pictures with *strong emotional content* are likely to be effective.

(5) *Suggestiveness.* The type of rumor which merely hints or suggests something instead of stating it is well adapted to spreading fear and doubt. The listener should always be allowed to formulate his own conclusions.

(6) *Concreteness.* The more concrete and precise a rumor, the less likely it is to become distorted in transmission.

OSS so sophisticated its rumor-mongering that, by 1944, it put them into formal subcategories. Some examples:

The CONFUSION RUMOR

Fear of inflation is the straightest and surest road to inflation. Working on this principle, OSS's Morale Operations floated three rumors:

• "The *Reichsdrucherei* [the German Mint] is printing large quantities of currency."

• "The value of the [German] mark in the black markets of Switzerland has dropped considerably."

• "Life insurance companies have asked the [German] government for extensive emergency loans. Because of the large number of deaths in the Reich, these companies are no longer solvent."

The DECEPTION RUMOR

During the summer of 1944, marketplace rumors were started

in Eastern Europe to the effect that the Germans were with-drawing German troops from the Crimea and leaving "all Roumanians behind to be annihilated." Within days, women staged a demonstration outside the Bucharest home of their president, shouting, "Send our husbands home."

The PERSONAL GOSSIP ATTACK RUMOR

OSS used many variations on the theme, "Where is Hitler?" OSS would state in its own broadcasts and through neutral press leaks that Hitler was expected to speak at such-and-such a Nazi anniversary observance. Such "commitments," of course, were solely of OSS's making. When Hitler did not appear, OSS would float reports of his "rumored death, disappearance, ill-ness, psychotic condition, or flight from the country." The aim was to "sow doubt in the minds of the public and the *Wehr-macht,* and cast suspicions on the motives and integrity of the Nazi leadership." These rumors so unnerved the Nazis that on December 29, 1944, the German propaganda minister Goebbels claimed over Radio Berlin that he had "purposely planted ru-mors that Hitler was ill as part of a deep and far-flung scheme to lull the Allies into complacency and set them up for the winter offensive." Goebbels's attempt to deflate the rumors told OSS that they were effective.

The HUMOROUS RUMOR

On June 16, 1943, OSS had its agents in occupied Europe float the quip, "Barbers in Holland are now charging five cents more for a shave, because German faces are longer these days." On August 25, 1943, feedback from the rumor was printed in the *Providence Journal:* "A Dutch underground newspaper reports that the barbers of Germany are now charging five cents exta each to shave Nazis because their faces are longer these days."

The PIPE-DREAM RUMOR

These rumors promised a better life to Axis soldiers who left the war. One, aimed at Germans in North Africa, was that POWs captured in the Middle East lived lives of pleasant activ-ity, and were used as chauffeurs for Allied generals. Several captured German airmen inquired about such assignments. They were disappointed.

The BOGEYMAN RUMOR

Harking to a past war, British intelligence (with OSS help) broadcast that the German navy would be ordered to make a final suicidal attack against the British. Historical precedent gave credibility both to the rumor and its intended effect. World War I reports of such a happening caused a German navy mutiny. World War II ended before this particular rumor had any effect.

The WEDGE-DRIVING RUMOR

These are nasty, for they exploit religious, racial, and other prejudices. Two of uncountable hundreds from OSS files:

● "At a dinner recently held at Karin Hall by Goering, beer was served in sacred vessels looted from churches in Northern Italy."

● "To save time and space, Himmler has ordered no distinctions be observed in cremations of Protestant and Catholic air-raid victims."

RUN DOWN A CASE

The decision to halt an operation involving a double agent, usually because of suspicions that the other side has become aware of the deception.

RUSSIAN INTELLIGENCE SERVICES (RIS)

The term used within CIA to denote the two major Soviet intelligence services, KGB and GRU. RIS began as a CIA acronym for Russian intelligence services in West Germany during the 1950s. It proved to be a local term that never "took" at Agency headquarters but was much used in the field. The more accurate designation would have been SIS, for "Soviet Intelligence Services," but the British pre-empted this label when MI6, the foreign intelligence service, became the Secret Intelligence Service. Courteously, CIA let the Brits have the initials SIS. (Secret Intelligence Service, in general usage, had about as much success as the attempt of New York City to rename Sixth Avenue "The Avenue of the Americas." In intelligence circles, one seldom hears anything of SIS or Secret Intelligence Service; the reference unfailingly is to MI6.) *(See also* ORGANS.*)*

S

SAFE HOUSE

A house or apartment rented by a person with no discernible connection to an intelligence agency and used for clandestine meetings with agents and other contacts. The normal guise—both for CIA and KGB—is a small apartment hired by an out-of-town businessman who travels frequently and who needs a modest place for occasional overnights. The preferred location for CIA safe houses during the 1970s (and before) was in Washington, D.C., apartment buildings in the canyons of Connecticut and Massachusetts avenues, and in suburban Northern Virginia.

One problem endemic to safe houses is suspicious neighbors who mistake odd hours and sporadic traffic as evidence of smuggling, gambling, or vice operations. (A U.S. Army Counterintelligence Corps agent in Munich once put off an inquiring landlady by stating, yes, he indeed was a homosexual, and he *needed* the apartment; she raised the rent 50 marks but agreed to remain silent.) An agent can give a semblance of activity to a safe house by arranging for a constant flow of junk mail (clipping a postcard in *Fortune* that offers a hundred or more corporate annual reports) interspersed with an occasional personal letter.

During the late 1960s, custodians of one CIA safe house put it to frequent use with girlfriends, as a cost-effective alternative to motels in Northern Virginia. One of the girls, an Agency analyst, unthinkingly used the phone to call a parent long-distance. A fiscal clerk questioned the charge, made inquiries, and referred the matter to the Agency security office. A directive issued shortly thereafter warned that safe houses were to be used *only* for official business.

A prearranged safety signal—a drawn window blind, a flower

pot on the balcony, the positioning of a vase in a window—tells whether there is any possible danger in the meeting.

SCATTER MOVE
See COUNTERSURVEILLANCE.

SCHCHIT
A two-layered film developed by GRU that will "permit secret documents to be photographed at high exposure on top of innocuous snapshots," according to British intelligence expert Robert Moses. If the film happens to be processed by someone unwitting of its nature, only the holiday snapshots appear. (The word means "shield" in Russian.)

SCHPICK
Derogatory KGB term for a novice operative.

S.D.E.C.E.
Service de Documentation Exterieure et Contre-Espionage (pronounced "suh-deck"), the French agency that performs both intelligence and counterintelligence functions—generally under rules of its own making. *SDECE*'s reputation for ruthlessness makes it unpopular even with agencies of nations with which France is supposedly friendly. In the words of a retired American spook, *"SDECE* on an everyday basis makes Hoover's FBI look like an elementary school crossing patrol." *SDECE*'s most innovatively grisly stunt was its execution of the Algerian nationalist leader Muhammad Ben Bella—agents dropped him 20,000 feet into the Mediterranean from the plane that supposedly was returning him to his homeland under a pledge of secure travel. Ideologically adaptable, *SDECE* has performed equally efficiently under left, center, and right-wing governments.

SDECE's offices on the Boulevard Mortier overlook the public swimming pool in the Parc des Tourelles, hence another nickname for the French service—*la piscine,* for "the swimming pool."

SDECE's name has been changed by the Mitterand government to DGSE (Direction Generale de la Securitie Exterieure), but professionals still refer to it by the old name.

SECRET INTELLIGENCE SERVICE (SIS)

The historical name for the arm of British intelligence responsible for foreign espionage and operations; now known professionally and popularly as MI6. Not to be confused with "Soviet Intelligence Services." *(See also* RIS.)

SECURE TELEPHONE

A telephone connection equipped with scramblers or other devices so that conversations cannot be overheard.

SECURITY EXECUTIVE

The committee responsible for control of British MI5 during World War II. Headed by Lord Swinton, the Security Executive was created after Prime Minister Churchill sacked General Sir Vernon Kell as director of MI5. Churchill was bent on keeping the existence of the Security Executive secret; when several members of Parliament heard rumors of its creation, Churchill replied to Commons that the subject was "not fitted for public discussion." Privately, Churchill said he would challenge the patriotism of anyone who asked further questions, MP or not. Nothing further was ever said of the Security Executive, which to intelligence insiders soon came to be known as the "Swinton Committee" after its chairman.

SEKSOT

Russian for informer. Genrikh Grigorievich Yagoda, who ran the Soviet secret police (then the GPU) in the 1930s, once boasted, "We can turn anyone into a *seksot*. . . . Who is eager to die of hunger? When the GPU works over somebody in order to make him an informant, we already have him under our thumb, no matter how he struggles against it. We take away his job, he won't find another one without the secret agreement of our organs. And, above all, if a man has a family, wife and children, he is forced to capitulate quickly." The network of *seksots* permeates all of Soviet society, by testimony of defected intelligence officers.

SEKTOR

A section in the KBG central office that controls illegals working abroad, or those preparing for assignment.

SERVICE, The

KGB officers' nickname for their organization.

SETTER

A CIA mail-intercept project conducted in New Orleans in 1957 involving the screening and opening of first class international mail via New Orleans en route to and from South and Central America. SETTER started as a result of Congressional protests about the "venomous propaganda" passing through New Orleans. SETTER was abandoned within two and one-half weeks as worthless.

SEXPIONAGE

The use of lust as a means of gathering intelligence. Although the concept is as old as the urge itself, the term "sexpionage" comes from British journalist David Lewis, whose book by that title was published in 1976. "To use the double bed as a passport to indiscreet pillow talk is a technique of Biblical antiquity," Lewis wrote. "In the tenth century, B.C., the first recorded sex spy, Delilah, used her charms to destroy the Danite hero Samson." Beds have continued bouncing ever since, in the name of the national interest.

The *femme fatale* who seduces statesmen and generals in the service of her country is a cliché of pulp fiction—and a reality of modern intelligence. *All* intelligence agencies employ sex as an element of tradecraft. In some instances, a person is furnished with a sex partner as a means of keeping him or her happy (as was the case with the late President Sukarno of Indonesia during a state visit to the United States, and the defected Soviet diplomat Arkady Shevchenko in 1978; CIA found the latter's particular playmate, "Judy Chavez," through the Yellow Pages of the Washington telephone directory).

But sexpionage can also be a brutal form of blackmail used against persons of many sexual persuasions. An oft-repeated warning given Westerners of rank, traveling to Iron Curtain countries, is "Don't go to bed with *anyone* other than your spouse, regardless of the temptation." But Eros often conquers common sense (and especially when given a boost by John Barleycorn).

The most illustrious victim was Sir Geoffrey Harrison, British ambassador to the USSR, who was seduced by a chambermaid, photographed by KGB, and withdrawn from his mission. Uncountable lesser personages have fallen victim to the same sort of trap. Several United States military sergeants served long prison terms for what began as vodka-fueled escapades with complacent women in Moscow, Warsaw, and other Eastern European capitals. Faced with blackmail photos, they agreed to spy for the Soviet bloc. The friendly women, it proved, were what KGB and its subordinates call "swallows"—prostitutes who are programmed to seduce Westerners. (Male prostitutes, both straight and homosexual, are known as "swans.")

The Czechs' secret service seems particularly obsessed with the use of sex as an intelligence tool. Eva Bosakova, several times an Olympics winner in gymnastics, was called by Czech defector Josef Frolik "an agent of long standing, utilized primarily for the production of compromising films of a sexual nature." Jiri Mucha, the writer, was also an STB agent, according to Frolik, who was used "to compromise members of the Prague diplomatic corps [with] sexual orgies arranged in his apartment."

Elizabeth Dorhofer, a strikingly beautiful international airline hostess recruited by Czech intelligence in the early 1950s, used a unique approach to American officers from whom she sought information: she would casually hand them a calling card bearing her nude photograph, and suggest a "quiet meeting for a drink." She enjoyed wide popularity among American servicemen in West Germany before being caught and jailed for seven years. In the 1960s Czech intelligence, acting for KGB, even managed to find a woman who had been rocket expert Wernher Von Braun's wartime lover. The Czechs sent the woman to the United States, where she tried to persuade Von Braun to share military secrets with the Soviets "in the interest of world peace." Von Braun was not interested in either the woman or her proposal, and she was turned over to the FBI.

During the 1960s, the Canadian national hockey team defeated the USSR in the semifinals of a tournament in Prague. The Czech minister of interior (i.e., secret police boss) was so miffed that he ordered subordinates to summon "all the best-looking Prague hookers" to the Hotel International, where the Canadian team was staying. According to defected Czech agent Josef Frolik, "these hookers did such a job on the Canadian team that the next day in the finals, the Czechoslovakians very easily defeated them."

Sexual blackmail is also undertaken by Western agencies. In aptly named Operation DEEP ROOT, the Royal Canadian Mounted Police in 1968 managed to get photographs showing the wife of a Soviet diplomat having intercourse with a Canadian. RCMP agents tried to force the woman to become an informant; she refused and left immediately for Moscow.

Western agencies have their own swans. Colonel Oleg Penkovskiy, the Soviet defector-in-place, made no secret of his desire for complaisant female company during a debriefing trip to Paris. The British Intelligence Service obliged with several svelte English girls. "They did not just happen to be in Paris," acknowledges Greville Wynne, who handled Penkovskiy. "We had brought them. They had been carefully selected for their quality as good companions, their expense accounts were generous, and their sole duty was to look after the gentleman from Belgrade (as Penkovskiy was introduced) should he become lonely. [Penkovskiy] must be kept happy, but it was far too dangerous to allow him to pick and choose for himself."

Western services also make frequent use of homosexuals. As a BBC commentator during the 1930s, Guy Burgess often did odd jobs for the British Secret Intelligence Service. An open homosexual, Burgess was once instructed to befriend Edouard Pfeiffer, *chef de cabinet* to Daladier, the French prime minister. Burgess's specific role was to act as a conduit for secret messages between Daladier and British Prime Minister Neville Chamberlain, who wished to bypass his own Foreign Office.

Sexual misconduct can backfire on a spy in unexpected ways. Geoffrey Arthur Prime spied for the Soviets for years—undetected—while working for the British Government Communications Headquarters (GCHQ), passing highly sensitive information about reconnaissance satellites. Although British security did not know it, Prime had an uncontrollable sexual interest in very young girls. His suspicious wife, looking for evidence of his sexual philandering, ran across spy material—as well as naughty photographs of prepubescent girls. Prime is now serving a long prison term.

Through the mid-1970s, intelligence personnel of Western agencies were advised against extramarital sexual liaisons as a prophylactic against blackmail. Anyone caught in such an affair faced censure or even dismissal. But changing sexual mores eased the rule (although homosexuals, even when they openly declare their sexual preference, still face automatic dismissal).

Several prominent intelligence personalities openly defied the stricture. The late Allen Dulles, while director of Central Intelligence, was a notorious womanizer, to the exasperation of his wife. Mrs. Dulles once told a friend that for a while she bought an expensive piece of jewelry each time she learned of an affair. "I had to stop," she said, "because I was running through all the family fortune."

The threat of blackmail did not deter Roger Hollis, longtime head of the British MI5, from an affair with his secretary, Edith Valentine Hammond. The affair was common knowledge to other MI5 officers (and presumably KGB). In February 1968, some two years after Hollis's retirement, Mrs. Hollis sued for divorce on grounds of his adultery with Miss Hammond. Once the decree was granted, Hollis married his former mistress, and they lived together until he died in 1973.

SHAKING OFF THE DOGS

Losing a surveillance team. The subject darts out of a subway car or a bus just as it leaves; he enters a department store or other building with multiple exits; he suddenly reverses his course and walks right past the surveillance person. A CIA agent in West Berlin once disposed of a KGB surveillant by arising in a bar and shouting, "Take your goddamned hand off my knee, you pervert." The flustered KGB man fled into the night, and the CIA man went about his business.

SHAKING THE TREE

A counterintelligence term that covers a potpourri of techniques intended to bring a dormant investigation alive. The purpose is to provoke the opposition, either through disinformation or an arrest of a known agent; the opposition's panicky reaction in turn will provide further leads. For instance, word can be leaked that an agent under arrest is cooperating and giving names of other members of his ring. If a suspected accomplice bolts for the airport, he would have some interesting days ahead.

SHAMROCK

The systematic interception, by the National Security Agency, of millions of international telegrams sent to, from, or by way of the United States, between 1945 and May 1975. The original purpose of SHAMROCK was to obtain the enciphered telegrams of certain foreign targets. For three decades, NSA screened some 150,000 messages monthly, handled by RCA Global and ITT World Communications; Western Union International gave NSA a less thorough range of messages.

SHAVKI

"Trash-eating dogs," in Russian contraction; KGB term for low-level agents. Such a designation shows KGB's contempt for outsiders, a major flaw of Russian intelligence.

SHEEP DIPPING

Using a piece of military equipment (such as a helicopter) or a military person in an intelligence operation under civilian cover. In actuality, the equipment or person remains assigned to the military; any transfer is on paper only. For instance, CIA sheep-dipped much of the military equipment given to the *contras* fighting the Sandinista government in Nicaragua in the 1980s. In a nonmilitary context, sheep dipping refers to placing of agents in organizations in which they can become active, in order to establish credentials that can enable them to collect information of intelligence value on similar groups. For example, the agent might join a radical group in the hope that this membership would make him acceptable to a terrorist organization.

SHEPHERD

A KGB strong-arm man who accompanies Russians who travel abroad; their mission is not companionship, but to insure that the subject does not defect. If the subject does flee, the shepherd goes to Siberia, or worse; hence his dedication to his job. (*See also* NURSEMAIDS.)

SHIFR ODTEL

Soviet term for an expert code-breaker, a man capable of deciphering messages without benefit of computers.

SHOPPED

Assassinated. A British MI6 euphemism.

Another British usage is less drastic; someone who is "shopped" is betrayed to the police, rather than killed. ("Shopped," in this context, has been supplanted by another term, "to grass"; i.e., to inform, which has come from the long-raging Irish civil war.)

SHOPPING LIST

The Western industrial, electronic, and other technological equipment that the Soviet Union attempts to purchase or steal abroad on an ongoing basis. The shopping list is revised and updated at least annually. KGB and GRU keep the exact contents a close secret so as not to tip Western intelligence of their most urgent requirements.

SHOPWORN GOODS

A would-be defector's information, so dated or remote as to be worthless to the other side. The debriefing officers who screen a potential defector try to determine, as a first order of business, whether he has any useful intelligence in his baggage. That an agent or intelligence bureaucrat has slid down the ladder does not necessarily make him worthless. Some overt over-the-hill cases are given refuge because of the historical perspective they can give to past operations and policies. Others are valuable for propaganda purposes. (The British traitor Kim Philby, for instance, had no current intelligence information in 1963 when the Russians took him in; his value was publicity—the chance for the Communists to boast about one of Britain's top spymasters being their puppet for years.)

Economics alone dictate that an intelligence service not accept willy-nilly any defector who sidles into an embassy. The initial debriefing expenses are only a minor part of the cost. The defector must be relocated under a new identity and given enough training so that he can earn a living; for the first months, at least, he is guarded. At one time the standard CIA arrangement was for a defector to become an Agency "consultant" for a number of months; after the stated period lapsed, he was on his own.

The British SIS in the postwar years went so far as to judge its defectors as "grade-one" and "grade-two." The latter were generally low-grade minor officials from East Europe, chiefly non-Communist, who either did not like the new Soviet regimes or had had some past connection with British intelligence. The system originally permitted them to enter Britain and stay, but gave them minimal or no other assistance. The Labour Government of Clement Attlee told SIS in the late 1940s that Britain was being flooded with shopworn goods, that the Eastern Europeans could do little of value; that henceforth they would not be granted political asylum simply because they were anti-Communist. SIS bided its time. When the government changed, SIS, and not the leftist Foreign Secretary Ernest Bevin, once more made decisions about which defectors should be given sanctuary.

SHOTGUN

A backup person who checks for surveillance when a case officer meets an agent under risky circumstances. The "shotgun" can also be used as muscle to detain an agent if he acts suspiciously. A CIA term.

SIBLINGS

CIA term for agents of the (sometimes rival) Defense Intelligence Agency.

SIGNATURE

The individual touch used by a wireless radio operator which indicates his personal transmitting pattern. The operator has a certain interval between words and characters, he commences and ends his messages in a characteristic manner, and his touch and speed are as different from another radioman's as are his fingerprints or voice. To an experienced monitor, a change in the signature is as obvious as would be a change in the sender's voice.

SILENT SCHOOL

Individual instruction at an intelligence school, so as to avoid exposing an agent who will work under deep cover to any other persons, save the essential trainers. (KGB term.)

SINGLETON

An individual agent operating alone, rather than as a member of a net or through a chain of intermediaries. Although frequently valuable for one-time in-and-out missions, the long-range value of such solo operators is doubted by intelligence professionals. The most famed singleton ever to don cloak and dagger was the fictional James Bond. In the words of one of novelist Charles McCarry's spooks, the singleton "requires no support . . . he operates alone, goes where he pleases." (McCarry worked for CIA before becoming a successful professional writer.) A unilateral, as distinguished from a singleton, works under agency control. *(See also* UNILATERAL.*)*

SINON

A Greek who was perhaps the first secret agent in history. He conceived the famous coup in Troy in which soldiers hid inside a wooden horse and were wheeled inside closely guarded gates.

SKATOL

A chemical in powdered form, developed by FBI laboratories, that emits an "extremely noxious odor rendering the premises surrounding the point of application uninhabitable." One use the FBI made of Skatol was to foul the San Diego printing plant that produced *The Black Panther,* newspaper of the extremist Black Panther Party. *(See also* WHO, ME?*)*

SKUNK WORKS

A secret section of the Lockheed Aircraft plant at Burbank, California, where CIA's Kelly Johnson developed the U-2 spy plane. Working with an unlimited budget and on a tight schedule, Johnson used unorthodox techniques to design and build the weird plane, which snooped at will over the Soviet Union for two years before the Gary Francis Powers incident.

SLEEPER AGENT, SLEEPER

An agent put into a circumstance or situation where his sole job is to wait until it becomes possible for him to actively gather intelligence, regardless of the length of time required. The most famed sleeper story, one taught as a textbook case for years at intelligence schools, proved apocryphal once World

War II documents were declassified. But the yarn, although bogus, does illustrate the principle: The Germans in the 1920s sent an agent to a coastal village near Scapa Flow, the vital British naval base. The agent worked as a watchmaker until 1939; when the war erupted, he provided information that enabled a German submarine to slip past nets and torpedo HMS *Ark Royal.* According to German intelligence files, no such sleeper existed.

A favorite "what-if?" game among CIA people concerns placing a sleeper in the USSR Politboro itself. If such did happen, what information would warrant the agent to risk blowing his cover? The consensus: nothing less than a warning of imminent war.

A sleeper is also referred to as a "back marker," or as "on ice."

SLUG
See SWALLOW.

SLUZHBA A
Russian for "Service A," an independent component within the First Chief Directorate of KGB, charged with overall management of "active measures" throughout the world.

SMERSH
The secret police units assigned to the Red Army that watch closely for signs of dissent or defeatism, created during World War II by Lavrenti Beria. Western intelligence agencies long attributed the word "smersh" to an acronym for *smert shpionam,* or "death to spies." But Kirill Khenkin, in his book *Okhotni, vverkh nogami (Hunter Upside Down),* published in Frankfurt, says the acronym was derived from the phrase *spetsial'nie metodi razoblachenia schpinov,* which means "special methods for exposing spies." Whatever the origin of SMERSH, the fictional character James Bond fought the mysterious group for the better part of his career.

SNAKE-EATER
Military term for a member of the Special Forces, or "Green Berets," specially trained for commando and other missions be-

hind enemy lines. As part of their training, Green Berets learn to eat what is available; hence their jungle diet often features reptilian cuisine.

SNITCH JACKET

Neutralizing a target by labeling him as a snitch, or informant, so that he would no longer be trusted. Methods utilized range from having an authentic informant start a rumor about the target member, to anonymous letters or phone calls, to faked informants' reports. If a number of persons from a target group are taken into custody, for instance, one of them might be held several hours longer than the others, then word floated that "[subject] decided to cooperate with the cops." Such is dangerous stuff, for the person accused of being a snitch could be killed. However, despite wide use of the snitch jacket technique during COINTELPRO, the FBI claimed to the Church Committee that no one was murdered.

SNUGGLING

A black propaganda technique. A clandestine radio program is broadcast on a frequency just adjacent to that of a "legitimate" station—say, that of a state-run broadcasting service. Listeners think they are hearing an official broadcast rather than artfully constructed propaganda. The British pioneered snuggling during World War II. CIA made most effective use of snuggling during the 1954 overthrow of the Marxist government of Guatemala. Under direction of CIA wizard David Atlee Phillips, rebel "announcers" broadcast such alarming items as, "It is *not* true that the waters of Lake Atitlan have been poisoned." Unwary listeners would think they were hearing a government broadcast and not believe the denial. Within hours, thousands of persons thought that the lake indeed had been poisoned.

SOFT FILES

Officially, soft files do not exist. Actually, these are maintained by every agency in the American intelligence community. They are devoted to personal information about officials and employees—sex and drinking habits, unusual hobbies or pastimes, dubious friends and associates. Because of their unof-

ficial nature, such files are not apt to be delivered in response to
a court or Congressional subpoena, or even by order of the
President. One former CIA executive called them "material essential to good management—you know this stuff before someone else does, and you act accordingly."

SOFT TARGETS
Friendly or neutral nations in which CIA has only a routine
interest in terms of intelligence coverage. For instance, the CIA
station in Stockholm would report on Soviet attempts to steal
Western technology and monitor political developments. But
activities would largely be confined to reporting. (See also HARD
TARGETS.)

SOLD
An agent who has been deliberately betrayed by his own
side.

SOSED
Neighbor, in Russian, meaning a complementary intelligence
service; KGB, for instance, would consider GRU or the Bulgarian service *sosed*.

SOUND MAN
Wiretapping or bugging expert.

SOUND SCHOOL
The FBI course in surreptitious bugging and wiretapping,
taught at the bureau laboratory in Washington.

SPLIT
KGB term for forcing a confession. "Forcing" carries its own
description.

SOURCE PROTECT
A warning phrase at the start of a communication that directs
that the contents be tightly guarded, even within the receiving
office. Since intelligence agencies operate on a need-to-know
basis, with compartmentalization of information, a distant of-

fice is often unaware of an ongoing operation. If events compel the second office to take control of the case on short notice, a fairly complete case history must be forwarded for guidance. "Source protect" is intended to alert the receiving office that the case is sensitive.

SOUTH CAFETERIA

CIA's "classified" dining area. Covert employees eat there, secure in the knowledge that no outsiders are permitted inside. Visitors from the "outside"—including such fellow spy agencies as the Defense Intelligence Agency and the National Security Agency—are shunted to the overt cafeteria. The food reportedly is better in South Cafeteria.

SOVBLOC GREEN

Officers and agents of MI6 who are not known to Soviet intelligence services. Hence they can be used on covert missions to Communist bloc nations.

SOVBLOC RED

MI6 officers and agents who are known to Soviet and bloc intelligence services and who are not eligible for clandestine assignments abroad. Their personnel dossiers carry the *SovBloc Red* stamp.

SOVETSKYAYA KOLONIA (SK)

The "Soviet colony," a catchall phrase covering all Soviets living in a foreign country or city under official or business cover. Each person in the SK is kept under KGB surveillance. KGB has the responsibility of protecting the SK against penetration by Western intelligence agencies. KGB's first line of defense in this regard is to discourage, if not outright prohibit, any contacts with Westerners outside the normal course of business; dependents and low-level personnel, for instance, are seldom permitted to leave the official compound.

In Washington, the main Soviet complex is a grouping of ugly stone buildings on a slight rise on Tunlaw Road Northwest, just west of Wisconsin Avenue. Iron fences topped with electronic devices surround the area, and on sunny days women and children mill around the grounds in a manner mindful of animals in a zoo. When the compound was under construction, residents of nearby apartment buildings complained that electronic interference was wreaking havoc with radio and TV reception, an indication that either (a) CIA and the FBI were packing the new building with surreptitious listening devices or (b) that KGB was packing the new building with surreptitious counterlistening devices. In any event, the noise cleared up soon after the Soviets occupied the building.

SPECIAL CATEGORY ITEMS FILE

Depository for the occasional embarrassing mail intercepts CIA made under its HTLINGUAL project. In March 1971, CIA agents opened and photographed a letter from Senator Frank Church, a member of the Senate Foreign Relations Committee (and later chairman of the select committee on intelligence that bedeviled CIA, the FBI, and other agencies). One alarmed supervisor suggested that any such intercepts not be put into Agency files and that mail screeners be ordered "to cease the acquisition of such materials." A formal directive in 1971 instructed HTLINGUAL teams not to watch-list or screen any mail from elected or appointed federal officials, or from senior state officials such as governors or lieutenant governors. If mail from such persons was accidentally intercepted, no reports would go to the central files; the letters themselves would go to a Special Category Items File maintained in the safe of the HTLINGUAL director. (That CIA did not simply order the destruction of such intercepts without further notice is indicative of the bureaucratic mind-set that occasionally grips the Agency. CIA was "most embarrassed" when it had to inform the hostile Church in 1974 that his mail had been read. That CIA did not try to conceal the episode is indicative of the show-it-all disclosure policy decided upon at high CIA levels when the Church probe began. Some outside friends felt this CIA attitude to be unbelievably dumb.)

SPECIAL INTELLIGENCE SERVICE (SIS)

An FBI unit created in 1940 to provide the State Department, the military, and other government agencies with intelligence from Latin America regarding "financial, economic, political and subversive activities detrimental to the security of the U.S."

SIS assisted several Latin nations "in training police and organizing anti-espionage and anti-sabotage defenses." Through SIS, the FBI remained dominant in Latin intelligence throughout World War II, resisting attempts of the rival Office of Strategic Services to operate there. FBI director Hoover so zealously guarded his assigned turf that he sabotaged an attempt by OSS to gain intelligence from the Spanish embassy in Washington. Hoover apparently decided unilaterally that, since both Latin Americans and Spaniards spoke the same language, he could claim Spain as "his." Hoover learned that OSS agents had broken into the embassy and photographed documents. Instead of registering a protest, he waited until OSS returned for a second surreptitious mission, then had FBI cars parked outside turn on their sirens. The OSS men scattered. The dispute reached the White House, where aides to President Roosevelt ordered OSS to turn over the Spanish embassy project to Hoover.

After the war a new agency, the Central Intelligence Group (predecessor to the CIA), was given responsibility for all foreign espionage and counterespionage operations worldwide. Hoover immediately disbanded the SIS; in some instances, SIS officers in the field burned their files rather than surrender them to the new agency.

Two other organizations with the "SIS" initials were noted earlier—the Soviet Intelligence Services and the (British) Secret Intelligence Service. Happily, no service now operates under such a designation.

SPECIAL OPERATIONS EXECUTIVE (SOE)

The British organization founded in 1940 to raise, arm, fund, and train resistance and partisan cadres in German-occupied territories in Europe. Prime Minister Winston Churchill instructed SOE to "Set Europe ablaze!" And that it did. SOE was first a trainer of, and then a parter with, the fledgling American Office of Strategic Services (OSS). SOE's ranks included professional soldiers, academics, and paroled jailhouse thugs. *(See also* STATELY 'OMES OF ENGLAND.)

SPECIAL TASKS

KGB euphemism for murders, kidnappings, and sabotage. These operations are conducted by "mobile brigades" created to carry out assassinations outside the USSR. The mobile groups were created circa 1936 by Nikolai Ivanovich Yezhov, then the Soviet secret police chief. The most famed (of many) victims was Leon Trotsky, axed to death in suburban Mexico City in 1939. Special tasks are now mostly delegated to subservient services such as the Bulgarian secret police. *(See also* MOBILE BRI-GADES.)

SPETSBURO

The Bureau of Special Tasks, the Soviet intelligence unit responsible for assassinations. The *Spetsburo* was responsible for the murders of many anti-Soviet Russian emigres in Western Europe during the 1940s and 1950s. Hiring on for murder is too much for even some hardened Soviet agents to stomach. On at least two occasions, agents of *Spetsburo* defected when ordered to kill specific persons. *Spetsburo* works under direct control of the Central Committee of the Communist Party.

SPIKED

A telephone or room that is bugged.

SPIKE MIKE

See PROBE MICROPHONE.

SPOOK

A term meaning "CIA officer" that originated in the American diplomatic corps—"sometimes pejoratively, sometimes affectionately," in the words of former CIA operative David Atlee Phillips. As Phillips noted in his memoir, *Night Watch*, "CIA officers have learned to live with the term, and occasionally refer to themselves as spooks."

SPOTTER

See SURVEILLANCE.

SPY

The intelligence historian Donald McCormick (who writes under the pen name Richard Deacon) traces the term to the ancient Chinese, where a single character in the Chinese language "had as its original meaning . . . that of a 'chink,' 'a crack,' or crevice." McCormick wrote (in his *Who's Who in Spy Fiction)* that "from any of these meanings one can derive the sense of a peep-hole, so it would seem that the earliest Chinese conception of a spy is very simply one who peeps through a crack."

The *Encyclopedia Britannica,* in its 1771 edition, defined a spy as "A person hired to watch the actions, motions, etc., of another; particularly of what passes in a camp. When a spy is discovered, he is hanged immediately."

SPY WEDNESDAY

The Wednesday before Good Friday, the day Judas agreed with the Romans that he would betray Jesus. Also the name of one of the best espionage novels ever written, by former CIA officer William Hood (Norton, 1986).

SQUIRT TRANSMITTER

A device that permits an agent operating in enemy territory to punch coded messages on a tape. Through the use of a special keying device, the tape can be fed through a radio transmitter at upwards of three hundred words per minute, enabling the agent to send his message rapidly and be off the air before directional radio honing equipment can locate him.

SSD (Staatssicherheitsdient)

State Security Service, the East German political police. Low-grade, used for border duty chiefly; untrusted by KGB overseers. Western agencies call *SSD* men "rent-a-cops." *SSD* is noted for bravery chiefly when given the chance to club unarmed border crossers, particularly women.

STAG

FBI code for its "Student Agitation" files.

STATE COMMITTEE FOR COORDINATION OF SCIENTIFIC RESEARCH WORK

The Soviet agency, tightly controlled by KGB, that handles all scientific and technical liaison activities with foreign countries. One major function is the recruitment of foreign scientists to act as spies; hence the procurement of scientific information and equipment. Because of the euphemistic title, the "coordination" committee often dupes Western scientists into believing it is in fact an independent scientific group. But Colonel Oleg Penkovskiy, the intelligence officer working for the committee when he began supplying information to CIA, testified that it, in fact, was a spy group.

STATELY 'OMES OF ENGLAND

Derisive name given to the Special Operations Executive (SOE), the British sabotage organization during World War II, prompted by the organization's proclivity for commandeering lavish country houses for training sites and operational bases.

STB (Statni Tajna Bezpecnost)

The Czech intelligence service. In Western lore, STB has "the longest legs of any Bloc service." Why? "Because they have to spread their legs the widest for KGB. The exercise made their legs grow."

STAY-BEHIND NETS

Clandestine infrastructures of leaders and equipment trained and ready to be called into action as sabotage and espionage forces, generally in areas subject to enemy occupation. Organizing stay-behind nets was William Colby's first assignment when he joined CIA in November 1950. (He served with OSS during World War II, then worked as a lawyer.) CIA feared the Soviets would use the Korean War, just under way, as a pretext for grabbing all of Western Europe. So Colby, who did guerrilla operations in Norway for OSS, was assigned to establish covert stay-behind nets in Scandinavia that would resist the Soviets should they indeed invade.

Radio transmitters, weapons, safe houses, trusted agents and handlers, codes—even recordings of national music to be played over clandestine radio stations—are the stuff with which stay-behind nets are equipped. Even a friendly host government is frequently unaware of the covert apparatus set up on its borders and manned by its citizens.

STAYER
A KGB deep-cover agent working in a foreign country whose only intelligence activity is to verify the safe arrival of other Soviet operatives assigned to the country. For instance, if KGB sends an agent into the United States under the cover of, say, a reporter for a British newspaper, the stayer would screen him from afar, then make contact via a previously arranged code phrase. The stayer enables the new agent to avoid any contact whatsoever with his nation's more conventional intelligence apparatus.

STERILE TELEPHONE
A telephone whose location cannot be traced, even through the telephone company. CIA has access to such telephones both in the United States and abroad, through techniques that go beyond bribery.

STERILITY CODING
The use of intermediary companies or individuals to cover purchases or payments that an intelligence agency does not wish to be traced to its own doorstep. Past uses include prostitutes for the late President Sukarno of Indonesia during a visit to the United States, and swift boats for anti-Castro Cuban exile groups. The amount and date of the expenditure will appear on the agency's books, its only stated purpose being the sterility code, the meaning of which is contained in a tightly held file elsewhere.

STOOGES
Low-level informants infiltrated into British POW camps during World War II to garner information on German and Italian prisoners. Stooges worked under the control of the "B"—or counterespionage—division of MI5.

STRINGER
A low-level agent who lives or works in proximity to an intelligence target and who passes along whatever information is acquired in the course of daily business. Stringers generally receive only rudimentary training and are paid a minimal stipend plus an occasional bonus for outstanding work. (The bo-

nus, however, is frequently paid *not* for valuab!e information, but for trivia; to do otherwise would pinpoint the sort of intelligence being avidly sought, an unacceptable security breach. But the bonus payments keep the stringer active.) Stringers are also used for such occasional odd jobs as serving as "live" letter-drops, renting a one-time-use safe house, or aiding in a hurry-up surveillance.

The stringer in all probability does not know the true identity of the intelligence service for which he is working; in West Germany in the 1950s, for instance, CIA agents routinely passed themselves off as agents of the U.S. Army's Counter Intelligence Corps (CIC). CIC agents took the guise of operatives from either the British Secret Intelligence Service (which employs enough linguistic oddballs to make the cover plausible) or the West German Gehlen Organization. Stringers are an expendable asset: If a double agent needs "credits" to establish his worth, stringers are the first to be exposed.

STUDY CIRCLES, STUDY GROUPS

The euphemism for the Communist cells that seeded the United States government during the 1930s, particularly in Washington. In addition to listening to lectures on Marx, Russia, and capitalism, many members of the study group were persuaded to steal papers, take home secret documents for copying, and allow Soviet handlers to set up photo workshops in their homes. By the testimony of Whittaker Chambers, one of the overlords of these groups, no less than seventy-five government employees were involved in Soviet espionage in 1936–38.

SUBMERGE

To disappear from sight once within the target country, usually to reappear later with new identification papers, cover story, and physical appearance.

SUCKING DRY

Soviet term for debriefing an agent after he returns from a mission.

SUITABILITY FILES

Highly personal information that might show the unreliability or vulnerability of a federal employee—with an intelligence or defense agency—which could lead to compromise of classified information. The information is highly personal (sexual proclivities, drinking habits, financial and marital disclosure). The National Security Agency states that it maintains suitability files to aid in providing counsel and other forms of guidance to individuals with personal problems—not to damage or threaten them. Even the highly suspicious Church Committee concluded it "has no reason to believe that information in these files has been misused."

SUPER-GRADER

In CIA parlance, a senior officer with a civil service rank of GS-16 or above. Although CIA employees are not members of the civil service system, they do work in the normal government grade structure, with GS-18 being the highest rank. Super-graders are the equivalent of flag officers (generals or admirals) in the military services.

SURFACING

Publicizing a defector, either through a carefully sanitized article or through a public press conference. Understandably, a defector is not surfaced until his interrogators have extracted all information of an intelligence value. Surfacing gives an agency the opportunity to "rub the other side's nose in it."

Surfacing can be posthumous, as was the case for Colonel Oleg Penkovskiy, the scientific intelligence officer who worked for CIA from April 1961 through August 1962. The Soviet state publishing house distributed some 10,000 copies of the transcript of Penkovskiy's trial, denouncing him as a vile traitor. CIA had the last word, however, with *The Penkovskiy Papers,* an amalgamation of reports, background material, and other information that was put into book form by Time-Life writer Frank Gibney.

SURREPTITIOUS ENTRY

FBI term for warrantless entries into a target property, both for installation of microphones and theft (and/or photography) of documents. *(See also* BLACK BAG JOB.)

SURROUND

Heavy-handed surveillance in which no precautions are taken to conceal the fact that a subject is being watched. When an agent realizes that he is surrounded, his hours of freedom are few.

SURVEILLANCE

Following a subject of intelligence interest, either by foot or by vehicle. A surveillance can be either "loose" with the watchers keeping such a distance that they do not risk detection themselves, or "tight," in which instance they do not break contact, even if spotted.

Sir Robert Baden-Powell, a turn-of-the-century British intelligence officer (and the founder of the world Boy Scout movement), didn't feel that surveillance of suspected agents was overly difficult. "Spies betray themselves by their walk," Baden-Powell once wrote. "A spy may effect a wonderful disguise in front yet be instantly recognized by a keen eye from behind. This is a point frequently forgotten by beginners." Fortunately for the British services, Baden-Powell progressed further in scouting than he did in intelligence.

"Spotters" are helpful in evading surveillance by automobile. A person who wishes to shake off tails drives around a traffic circle two or three times. A couple sits in a parked car on the circle. If after his second or third circuit no tail appears, the woman draws a scarf around her head, or the man takes off his hat—a "clear signal." A bridge can be substituted for the traffic circle. Many persons who work covertly for CIA routinely take two sweeps across Memorial Bridge in Washington before proceeding out the George Washington Parkway to Agency headquarters; circles at either end make turnarounds easy.

SVOI

Russian for "he is one of us," meaning in intelligence terms a witting collaborator. Its use indicates a willingness to submit to orders and discipline. Another Russian term, *nashi,* has a parallel meaning.

SVYAZNA

In Russian, "cut-out."

SVYAZNIYE

In Russian, "go-between"—a functionary who makes direct contact with agents and thence with KGB agents assigned to a Soviet embassy.

SW (Secret Writing)

Writing modified, usually by chemical means, to remain invisible.

SWALLOW

A female KGB spy. The Russian word for swallows is *lastochki*. Despite specific warnings, U.S. embassy personnel in Moscow maintain a fatal affinity for offered Soviet flesh. KGB procedure is to exact payment once the target has returned to the United States—that is, "if you don't spy for us, interesting pictures and recordings will be sent to your wife and mother." Mythology is that KGB swallows are trained at a special "sex school." In actuality, the swallows attend a rather basic intelligence school, and sexual prowess does not figure in the curriculum. A swallow, in essence, is a prostitute with an IQ slightly above her sisters-on-the-street. Swallows are viewed with utter contempt both by fellow KGB agents and CIA officers against whom they are directed on occasion. *(See also* SEXPIONAGE.)

SWALLOW'S NEST

An apartment or house used by a swallow (see above) for the sexual entertainment of a KGB target. The "nest" is fitted with audio and video recording equipment to put the target's sexual play onto permanent record, for use in blackmail.

SWIM

The dispatch of a KGB officer from the USSR to an assignment abroad. For example, "Boris is going to swim to London."

SYMBOL NUMBER

An FBI code number used in lieu of the words "telephone surveillance" as a cover for a wiretap.

t

TALENT-SPOTTER

A deep-cover agent responsible for spotting persons who are suitable recruits for intelligence work. The label is most commonly used to denote someone who recruits agents to work against their own country (most vividly illustrated in the instance of the Cambridge don who persuaded numerous undergraduates to become Soviet agents in the 1930s. The most famous of his "talents" were Kim Philby, Donald Maclean, Guy Burgess, and Anthony Blunt). The same term is applied, in a positive sense, to American university professors who look for students with the attributes essential to a CIA officer.

A skilled talent-spotter works indirectly: Seldom does he state at the outset exactly what he expects of the target. Anthony Blunt, under interrogation, quoted the approach used on him by Guy Burgess: "Anthony, we must do something to counter the horrors of Nazism. We can't just sit here and talk about it. . . . I am already committed to work secretly for peace. Are you prepared to help me?" Only later was the recruit informed he was working for the Comintern and for Soviet intelligence.

TANK, THE

A sound-secure room in the larger CIA stations around the world. Novelist David Wise described the London tank in his book, *Spectrum:* "The tank, which resembled a streamlined railroad car on stilts, was actually a room within a room. It rested on steel legs above the floor. A speaker had been mounted on the outside, and when the tank was in use, a noisemaking tape emitted a loud, steady sound of whirring machinery." (A tape of a cotton mill in North Carolina, according to station lore.)

Tanks are bugproof—but also windowless; they tend to get stuffy.

TARGET STUDY

A compilation of all available information on a person being considered for recruitment as an intelligence source. Sources include existing file material, surveillance for as long as two months to check the person's associations and movements, and whatever information can be garnered from other intelligence agencies. The "vulnerability paragraph" of the target study outlines why the person might be receptive to an offer to work for a foreign intelligence agency—money, ideology, vulnerability to blackmail; the reasons are limitless.

TASK

An assignment for intelligence personnel.

TASS

The official Soviet news agency, whose correspondents abroad double as espionage agents. Although TASS "reporters" protest their independence of government control, on at least one occasion they have been forced to fly their true colors. In 1949 a TASS reporter somehow became president of the Foreign Press Association in London, a position for which government officials are not eligible. A Czech refugee named Krajina, living in London, claimed he had been libeled in a TASS dispatch and filed a civil action in court. The Soviet embassy intervened with a declaration that the TASS employees were Russian officials and hence entitled to diplomatic immunity. A British appeals court upheld the Soviet position—but in doing so shattered the myth of TASS "independence."

In Washington, TASS correspondents enjoy many of the same privileges as do American reporters. But there are exceptions: TASS men, for instance, are not included in the "deep background" sessions at which officials, such as the Secretary of State or Defense, explain policy issues off-the-record. Further, TASS employees are subjected to the same FBI surveillance as are formal members of the Soviet diplomatic mission.

TAYNIK (or *Tainik)*
See DUBOK.

TECHNICAL COVERAGE
FBI euphemism for a wiretap or bug.

TECHNICAL SERVICES
The division of MI5 responsible for electronic and other forms of nonhuman surveillance.

TECHNOLOGY COLLECTION OFFICER
A KGB or GRU agent assigned to steal or buy Western technology, either in the form of plans or actual working items. Since the late 1970s, the Soviet emphasis has been on computer and microchip technology. Technology collection officers work under the Directorate of KGB (more formally, the Scientific and Technical Directorate). The department known as "Line X" is specifically responsible for foreign field operations.

TECHNOLOGY TRANSFER ASSESSMENT CENTER
A CIA branch that documents the use the Soviet Union and its allies make of technology acquired from the West; also, the clandestine methods used to obtain the items. During 1983–'84, according to William J. Casey, director of Central Intelligence, the center played a role in the expulsion of "well over 150 Soviet agents" from 20 countries for "technology theft." Casey noted in a 1984 speech, "Successes have also been achieved in recovering stolen technology, blocking shipments, and breaking up the technology smuggling rings."

TELEGRAPH
A prearranged signal that tells an agent he should pick up material from a "dead drop." Reino Hayhanen, a Soviet spy in the United States from 1952 through 1957, used as his telegraph to other agents a childlike chalk scrawl on a wooden fence. Hayhanen came to the United States under deep cover, posing as the American-born son of Estonian parents who had taken him to Estonia before World War II. He defected to American

intelligence in 1957. His information led, in turn, to the seizure of Colonel Rudolf Abel, the highest-ranking spy ever caught in the West.

TELL-TALE

A form of talcum powder, invisible on white paper; examination under an ultraviolet light will reveal whether the documents on which it is placed have been disturbed.

TERMINATE WITH EXTREME PREJUDICE

Murdering an agent who has outlived his usefulness, per spy novelists and movie writers. The term has never been used by any intelligence professional, espionage mythologists notwithstanding. *(See also* DISPOSAL, EXECUTIVE ACTION.)

TERRORISM

"The unlawful use of force or violence against persons or property to intimidate or coerce a government, the civilian population or any segment thereof, in furtherance of political or social objectives." Such is the formal definition adopted by the FBI in 1982 and followed by other U.S. government agencies.

THIRD COUNTRY OPERATIONS

Using a base in one country as a means of gaining access to intelligence of other countries, and of conducting operations elsewhere in the geographical area. The host country is either friendly or neutral, and is itself of no special intelligence interest. Both the KGB and CIA use Mexico City as outpost for "third country operations" throughout Latin America and maintain large stations there. As a traditional haven for "political" exiles, Mexico hosts revolutionaries of every leftist hue, the one ground rule being that they do not get involved with local dissidents. Cuba's DGI *(Dirección General de la Inteligencia,* or General Intelligence Directorate) is prominent in Mexico because of the ease of travel to other Latin countries. As a resident journalist in Mexico City in the 1960s, I could make contact with Castroite groups with considerably more ease, say, than I could make a dental appointment.

TIRE SPIKE

A crude sabotage device developed by the OSS during World War II, still in wide use. The spike is a piece of one-eighth-inch-thick steel, cut in the form of a four-pointed star. The star is three inches in diameter, and the points are alternately bent up and down at an angle of 45 degrees from the horizontal. The tire spike is used to puncture rubber tires of vehicles or airplanes; it is most effective when scattered in the gravel or ruts of unpaved roads, or on airplane runways. Because of the angle in which the points are bent, one of the points will always be in a vertical position, regardless of how the spike is dropped.

OSS doctrine was for liberal use of the spikes, which were shipped to field units in 125-pound lots packed in wooden kegs (2,160 one-ounce spikes per keg).

The KGB and its subsidiaries have made frequent use of tire spikes to discourage surveillance or pursuit in operations involving cars. For instance, on July 8, 1952, Soviet agents grabbed the West German anti-Communist lawyer Walter Linse from a street near his home in a suburb of West Berlin. A brave citizen drove in chase, only to have his tires ruined by spikes thrown from the kidnap vehicle. Despite his flattened tires, the citizen pursued Linse's captors to the border of the Soviet zone —where guards raised the barrier gate with precision timing as the kidnap car roared into view.

"TONGUE," CAPTURING A

Soviet military intelligence term for kidnapping individual officers and enlisted men who are apt to have information of value. During World War II, tongue operations were conducted chiefly by partisan bands with Chekist advisors; among the tongues caught by these raiding groups was the German puppet minister of defense in Slovakia and the commander of the Slovakian land forces. In the postwar period, the Soviets frequently used kidnapping to silence enemies, particularly nationalist exiles from the Sovietized puppet regions within the USSR.

TONGUE-TANGLER

Speech alteration device developed by CIA's Technical Services Division. A thin layer of flesh-colored plastic, it causes the wearer to speak with a slight lisp. Normal speech intonations are also changed. The tongue-tangler is not popular because it is uncomfortable.

TOSS

To enter and search, surreptitiously (and perhaps illegally), the living quarters or office of a person who is a suspect in an espionage or criminal case.

TRADECRAFT

The methods by which an intelligence agency conducts its business. "Tradecraft may be mysterious to outsiders," writes CIA veteran William Hood, "but it is little more than a compound of common sense, experience, and certain almost universally accepted security practices. . . . The fact is that tradecraft is like arithmetic: it has been around for centuries. The basics are easy to learn and good texts can be found in any library. Although it is easy to make mistakes under pressure, only the advanced subjects—like multiplying fractions or manipulating double agents—are particularly complex."

Tradecraft can be learned in practical fashion. During World War II, David Atlee Phillips, an air force officer, escaped from a German POW camp. Making his way toward Allied lines, Phillips was helped by a friendly French farmer. "Give me your name and address," Phillips said, "I want to do something nice for you once the war ends." The farmer shook his head. "No," he said, "*you* give me *your* name and address." As Phillips commented later—after retiring from a quarter century service as one of CIA's top clandestine officers—"that was my first grass roots lesson in tradecraft. Had I been caught with the farmer's name in my pocket, he would have been a dead man."

TRAITOR

A person who sells or otherwise divulges his own country's secrets, be it for monetary or other reasons.

TREFF

A German espionage term, of World War II origin, meaning a meeting between an agent and his controller in a neutral country. *Treff* now is used widely by both Western and Soviet agencies.

By CIA practice, the first item discussed in a *treff* is the timing and location of the next meeting, in the event the meeting in progress must be broken off suddenly.

Good tradecraft calls for sensitive *treffs* to be made in a country where the agents do not live or normally work. For instance, KGB controls in London regularly meet British informers in France or Belgium, where close surveillance is more difficult.

TREE-SHAKER
See AGENT PROVOCATEUR.

TRIANGULATION
In signals intelligence, a technique of locating secret radio transmitters. Three radio receivers have revolving antennae that permit them to take bearings on a radio signal. The bearings are plotted on a map; their point of intersection gives the general locale of the radio. A mobile receiver (concealed in a van) then roams the locale until it is in audible proximity to the signal. The Germans used triangulation with deadly accuracy during the first part of World War II; "squirt transmissions" that were on the air for just minutes, or even seconds, helped counter the technique.

In counterintelligence, triangulation is a technique for locating the source of leaks of classified material. Classified information is put in reach of suspect persons; each receives it in slightly altered form (for instance, aircraft production figures are varied). "Feedback" as to what information is being leaked —obtained either by radio intercepts or human sources—points toward the persons who were entrusted with the specific figures divulged. In the next round, each of these persons is again given slightly variant forms of information. When the information emerges again, its source is usually evident. Triangulation is not unlike trout fishing: it requires a steady hand, patience, and the willingness to stand around in cold and uncomfortable water while waiting for something that might never happen.

TURN
To persuade an enemy agent to go to work for one's own intelligence service, either through persuasion or coercion. An agent so persuaded is said to be "turned."

TWENTY COMMITTEE
The British unit charged with convincing German intelligence during World War II that its Abwehr agents, although captured, were still actively spying. Through aggressive counterintelligence and radio intercepts, the British systematically caught every German agent dispatched to the United Kingdom during the war. The radios of many of these agents were used to send back spurious—but plausible—intelligence. Since the operation was a double-cross (XX), the British restated the Roman numerals as Twenty; hence the committee's designation.

TWISTED BALLS
According to Donald McCormick, in his *Who's Who in Spy Fiction*, "originally a Russian expression to indicate an agent who had at some time previously been given electric shocks in the genitals. Such a man was considered relatively an easy subject for further interrogation."

TWO GIRLS, THE
German Communist slang for the separate Soviet spy organizations working in their country before World War II. "Grete" was the KGB predecessor: "Klara" was the Red Army.

u

UNCLE
KGB, as referred to the Communist bloc intelligence services. For example, "Uncle is coming around tomorrow."

UNILATERAL
A CIA representative or source who operates in a foreign country without visible ties either to the Agency or the U.S. embassy. He might or might not be a formal employee. But his cover is constructed so that he can be officially disavowed if one of his operations goes awry. Unilaterals are used in risky recruiting efforts when the target is, say, an official of the host government and apt to complain if asked to supply information about his nation's politics. A unilateral differs from a singleton in that he works under Agency control; the latter is a freewheeler.

UNSUB
FBI abbreviation for "unknown subject." When the bureau opens a dossier on a person whose name it is unable to determine, he is given this designation plus a code affix—to wit, UNSUB JOHN.

USTASHA
A Croatian nationalist group of fascist origin, connected in recent years with KGB. *Ustasha* agitates for independence for the Yugoslav province of Croatia. KGB supports its activities as a means of punishing the Yugoslav regime for not swearing allegiance to the Soviet bloc. *Ustasha* territorists have gunned down and blown up numerous victims in Europe; they also claimed credit for a bloody 1975 bombing at LaGuardia Airport in New York.

V

VACUUM CLEANER

An informant who provides an intelligence agency with details of every aspect of the activities of a target organization, regardless of their relevance to his assignment.

VIDEM

FBI code for its "Vietnam Demonstration" security files.

VLADIMIR

A Soviet jail for important political prisoners, located 150 miles east of Moscow. Originally constructed by the czar in the 1910s, Vladimir became infamous as a way station for prisoners forced to march to the steppes and salt mines of Siberia, many hundreds of miles further east. KGB made it a major prison in the 1920s. A Russian saying has it that fortunate prisoners die before reaching Vladimir, the less lucky die thereafter, and the *really* unlucky make it to the salt mines. There is no recorded instance of a prisoner escaping from Vladimir and few instances where a person is released: if he survives his original term, he is simply resentenced. Some German and Japanese generals imprisoned soon after World War II were said to still be in Vladimir in the 1970s.

V-MEN

Agents of the West German Gehlen Organization who worked behind the Iron Curtain. Despite the illegality of their primary mission, the commercial firms which gave cover to V-Men were most proper in their daily operations: they obtained business licenses, they paid taxes, they insured their employees, and they registered their motor vehicles. They also grabbed up useful information by the crateful.

W

WALKERS

KGB term for low-level agents sent across the border between East and West Germany.

WALK-INS

Persons who volunteer their services to an espionage agency. Contrary to popular mythology, agencies in fact do accept such volunteers, and make wide use of them. In the words of former CIA operative William Hood, " 'It's the walk-in trade that keeps the shop open' is one of the first bits of operation wisdom that is impressed on newcomers to the business." While in Vienna in the 1950s, Hood was responsible for "running" one of the most valued walk-in informants ever recruited by CIA— Pyotr Popov, an officer of GRU, the Soviet military intelligence service.

Other walk-ins who have been valuable over the years include Fritz Kolbe, an anti-Nazi career diplomat in the German foreign office, who suddenly appeared at Allen Dulles's OSS office in Geneva in 1943; Oleg Penkovskiy, a Soviet scientific intelligence officer who sabotaged Khrushchev's attempt to frighten the United States out of Berlin in 1961; and Arkady Shevchenko, a top-level Soviet diplomat at the United Nations in the late 1970s.

Because intelligence agencies tend to be skeptical of volunteer defectors until they establish their *bona fides* (because of the ever-present danger of a double agent) walk-ins can have difficulty persuading anyone to take them seriously. The most extreme example involved Igor Gouzenko, who in 1945 was a GRU cipher clerk in the Soviet embassy in Toronto. Angered that the USSR was simultaneously taking Canadian aid and stealing their secrets, Gouzenko one night bundled up a suitcase of confidential dispatches, took them to a newspaper, announced he was defecting, and offered the story. As corroborating evidence, Gouzenko offered documents naming Canadian officials who were spying for the Soviets. "Come back tomorrow," a subeditor told him.

Gouzenko the next day visited other newspapers and a number of government agencies, but could persuade no one to listen to him or read his papers. Not until Soviet security officers wrecked his apartment that evening, in a search for the purloined documents, did officials recognize he was serious. His disclosures—the first hard evidence of the Soviets' cold war intentions—shocked Western nations. They also led to the cracking of a multi-nation spy ring stealing atomic secrets both in the United States and Great Britain, plus the arrests of Alan Nunn May, a British nuclear physicist, and Klaus Fuchs, a German-born British scientist. (Gouzenko thereafter lived in hiding —with a KGB price on his head; he died in 1982 at age 65.)

WALK-PAST

The appearance by an illegal agent working abroad, at a set time and place, so that he or she can be observed by an officer of the illegals' support staff working in the area. No contact is made. The walk-past enables the intelligence agency to know that the illegal has arrived and is ready to go to work. It also enables the support officer to check whether the illegal is under surveillance. The illegal might be required to do a walk-past in key cities en route to his ultimate destination; thus, if he is detected and arrested en route, his agency has at least a general idea of where his mission went awry.

WASH

The recycling of a valid passport—one obtained either by theft or purchase from a tourist—to remove all traces of writing and to reissue it with a new photograph and name. Penniless American students who sell their passports in Paris or the Middle East have unwittingly provided authentic cover for uncountable KGB agents. Since the 1970s, KGB technicians have also washed documents for use by the Palestine Liberation Organization and other international terrorist groups.

WATCHER SERVICE

The department of MI5 responsible for surveillance of suspects, either by car or on foot.

WATCH LIST

A compilation of names of persons considered of interest to the intelligence community. The most common usage is at border-crossing points. One's presence on a Watch List is not evidence of subversion or espionage, but only that the person named has contacts that deserve close scrutiny. For instance, a government officer in a sensitive job who regularly received mail with a return address known to be a KGB letter-drop could expect to have his life fairly closely monitored. The Secret Service maintains an extensive Watch List of persons considered threats to the President of the United States.

One Watch List detailed publicly was that of persons whose mail was to be given particular scrutiny during CIA's HTLINGUAL screening of mail to and from the Soviet Union, beginning in the 1950s. The criteria for inclusion on the Watch List were succinctly defined to include persons from the "Denied Area" of Europe (i.e., Soviet bloc nations) who had gone to work for CIA or other intelligence agencies; who had been repatriated to either the United States or Canada; who had or would return to the USSR or other Denied Areas; who were suspected Soviet intelligence agents resident in the U.S.; or who were foreign nationals from the USSR being utilized by CIA in any capacity. The original Watch List, of some twenty names, by 1956 had expanded to more than six hundred, with additions being suggested regularly by both CIA and FBI counter-intelligence officers. It came to include persons who had communicated with individuals already on the Watch List and those selected for scrutiny by random sampling of Soviet mail.

Between them, CIA and the FBI included on the Watch List such individuals and organizations as the American Friends Service Committee; authors Edward Albee and John Steinbeck; numerous scientific organizations and their members; and various political activists. One peculiar target was Frederick A. Praeger Publishers—which had produced many books with covert Agency support.

WEEDER

A security officer responsible for screening British state papers for embarrassing material—before they are put into the public record after passage of the statutory declassification period. One subject automatically excised—supposedly—is any mention of MI5 operations. There is an occasional slip. In early 1982, a careless weeder permitted passage of a document about illegal MI5 wiretaps of Frederick Kuh, late London correspondent of the *Chicago Sun,* that had been conducted in 1946, after he wrote a story about the government's atomic energy bill; and of Paul Enzig, political correspondent of the *Financial Times* of London, for a critical story on government economic planning. John Drew, former Cabinet functionary whose office handled the matters in the 1940s, was aghast when *The Economist* informed him his files were now in the Public Works Office in Kew. "This sounds really a bit near the bone," Drew said. "In fact, it's more than that: you're digging near the bone."

WEEDING

The process of reviewing files and discarding those no longer considered important enough to warrant storage space. Computerization of files in such agencies as CIA and DIA during the past few years means that file information is now retained permanently.

WESTPOINTER

A CIA mail intercept project based in San Francisco during brief periods between September 1969 and October 1971. Mail to and from a single Asian nation was examined—first, surface only; later, opened and photographed. In WESTPOINTER, postal officials were not privy to the fact that mail was being opened. CIA people would surreptitiously place envelopes in their pockets when no one was watching, and take the letters to a Technical Services Division laboratory in the San Francisco area for examination. Although the Church Committee report did not name the "Asian nation" targeted, the quoted memoranda suggested the People's Republic of China. (CIA's Plans Directorate, also involved in the project, code-named it KM-SOURDOUGH.)

WET SQUAD

A special KGB assassination group, controlled by and dispatched from KGB Central in Moscow. CIA credited the wet squad with no less than three assassinations of major Afghan leaders during the two years preceding the 1979 Soviet seizure of that country. Another victim was President Ahmed Hussein Ghashmi of North Yemen, a staunch foe of the Soviets. The method used in this instance was particularly dastardly. An envoy of the pro-Soviet rival state of South Yemen visited President Ghashmi, ostensibly to discuss peace. When he opened his briefcase, it exploded violently, blowing both envoy and Ghashmi to bits. CIA specialists said manufacture of such a sophisticated device was far beyond Yemeni capability; they concluded the incident was planned in Moscow and carried out via the wet squad.

WET WORK

An operation involving the shedding of blood. KGB term.

WHITE CROW

KGB term for someone who stands out in a crowd, a situation to be avoided by a covert agent.

WHITE INTELLIGENCE

Information gleaned from such overt sources as foreign publications and broadcasts. The United States Government Printing Office, which publishes hundreds of thousands of words annually on Congressional hearings on defense plans, has no counterpart in the USSR. The Soviet embassy in Washington receives some 1,700 pounds of mail daily, by FBI scales, the bulk of it governmental and other publications. Countless other pounds go to various KGB mail drops and convenience addresses around the country.

WHITE PROPAGANDA

Statements of publications that make no attempt to conceal authorship, source, or point or origin. (See also GRAY and BLACK PROPAGANDA.)

WHO, ME?

A "psychological harassing agent" the Office of Strategic Services developed for use in Asia during World War II. As an OSS manual stated, "It is to be squirted directly upon the body or clothing of a person a few feet away. The odor is that of Occidental feces, which is extremely offensive to Orientals. Very good use of this agent can be made by native patriots in crowded markets and bazaars to create disturbances, attack morale of enemy guards, and to divert attention from other activities." *Who, Me?* consisted of a soft metal tube with a screw cap on a projecting tip. When the cap was removed and the tube squeezed, it squirted a liquid chemical that OSS described as being of "violent, repulsive and lasting odor." *Who, Me?* tubes weighed half an ounce and were slightly less than three inches long; OSS distributed them five to a carton.

WICKET GATE

Soviet term, circa World War II, for a place where agents could cross a military front line into enemy territory.

WITTING

A person who knowingly cooperates with an intelligence agency. The word first came to public view in garbled form in the mid-1960s, when *Ramparts Magazine* exposed CIA links with the National Student Association. One of the magazine's informants said that NSA officers who knew of the arrangement were *"witty,"* and two decades later this corrupted version of *"witting"* still shows up in spy novels. *(See also* BIGOT, LIST, NOT WITTING.)

WOMEN SPOOKS

In spying, forget about women's lib. Under pressure, bureaucracies such as CIA, NSA, and DIA put women into responsible positions; their equal-opportunity officers can produce statistics showing "incredible gains." True in analytical and administrative areas; not so true in Clandestine Services. By definition, spies work abroad; few foreign countries would give credence to a woman traveling under a cover that would make her an effective operative. There are *notable* exceptions that CIA has not chosen to publicize—notable, however, means rare.

It is probable, however, that (at least in Western intelligence agencies) attitudes have progressed beyond those expressed by Richard Sorge, Soviet master spy in Japan before World War II, who once said: "Women are absolutely unfit for espionage work. They have little understanding of high politics or military affairs. Even if you use them to spy on their husbands, they do not really understand what their husbands are talking about. They are too emotional, sentimental and unreliable."

WORK NAME
An alias; CIA terminology.

WRATH OF GOD
An Israeli counterterrorist group formed after the massacre of Olympic athletes in 1972. "WOG"—also known as "Israel's long arm"—has as its mission to identify, search out, and destroy Arab terrorists in Europe; the chief target was the Black September Palestinian group which claimed credit for the Munich murders. In two years, Wrath of God killed more than a dozen Black September leaders. It was "officially" disbanded in late 1974 after Western European governments protested its freebooting activities within their boundaries. Whether WOG truly was disbanded is a matter of conjecture.

Y

YAVKA
Soviet name for a safe house.

YEZHOVSHCHINA
Russian for "The Great Purge," the period during the late 1930s when Stalin decimated Soviet society of its leading generals, scientists, physicians, and politicians. Named for the chief of Soviet state security, Nikolai Ivanovich Yezhov.

Z

Z-COVERAGE

The first and longest-running FBI mail intercept program, initiated in 1940 to cover Axis diplomatic offices in Washington. Z-Coverage later extended to diplomats of various Communist nations, with the purpose "to detect individuals in contact with these establishments who might be attempting to make contact for espionage reasons, for purposes of defecting, or who might be illegal agents."

Z-Coverage, as it evolved, aimed at tight targets, screening incoming mail in urban postal zones where foreign agents were believed to be living. According to Church Committee testimony, coverage included, at various times, postal zones 10023, 10024, and 10025 in New York; zone 48231 in Detroit and the suburban Hamtramck area; and, finally, all mail sent to San Francisco from New York and Washington.

The Z-Coverage was fruitful. In July 1964 the program intercepted a letter from "an employee of an American intelligence agency" to a foreign embassy in which he "offered to sell information relating to weapons systems . . . and also expressed an interest in defecting." Three illegal agents were detected in Washington alone. And Z-Coverage monitored the demands laid upon Chinese-born scientists who were ordered to return to the Mainland lest their relatives suffer reprisals. The queries sent to these scientists—information they were expected to bring back to the Mainland—alerted U.S. intelligence to the areas of particular interest to the Communist Chinese.

ZENITH TECHNICAL ENTERPRISES

Cover corporation for CIA's covert war against Castro Cuba during the early 1960s (code-named JMWAVE). Zenith was located on the University of Miami's South Campus, adjacent to

the abandoned Richmond Naval Air Station, mostly destroyed
by a hurricane; it supposedly did classified "government research." Zenith had the outward appearance of a functioning
business. A notice to salesmen, pinned on an outside doorway,
listed calling hours for various departments. On the wall of the
reception room was a certificate from the United Way thanking
Zenith for "outstanding participation" in its annual fund rais-
ing.

ZODIAC (for Spies)

Mercury is the most favorable planet for a spy, with Gemini
as the sign of the zodiac (birthdays May 21 to June 21). As an
astrologer told the British espionage expert Bernard Newman,
"Spies are significant in dreams. If you dream that you are a spy
in the service of your own country, this indicates that you will
be elected to some position you do not desire. If you dream that
you are being spied on, this is a warning to be more circumspect
in your behaviour."

Sources

Among the printed sources for *A Dictionary of Espionage* were the following volumes: Joseph Burkholder Smith, *Portrait of a Cold Warrior* (New York, 1976); Christopher Felix, *A Short Course in the Cold War* (New York, 1963); David Atlee Phillips, *The Night Watch* (New York, 1977), and *Careers in Secret Operations* (Frederick, Maryland, 1985); William Hood, *Mole* (New York: 1982); A. I. Romanov, *Nights Are Longer There* (Boston, 1972); E. Howard Hunt, *Give Us This Day* (New Rochelle, 1973); Harry Rositzke, *The KGB: The Eyes of Russia* (New York, 1981); David J. Dallin, *Soviet Espionage* (New Haven, 1955); Chapman Pincher, *Dirty Tricks* (New York, 1980), and *Too Secret Too Long* (New York, 1984); Donald McCormick, *Who's Who in Spy Fiction* (New York, 1977); Bradley Earl Ayers, *The War That Never Was* (Indianapolis/New York, 1976); James Bamford, *The Puzzle Palace* (Boston, 1982); Louise Bernikow, *Abel* (New York, 1970); Anthony Cave Brown, *Bodyguard of Lies* (New York, 1975); William Colby, *Honorable Men* (New York, 1978); Thomas Coulson, *Mata Hari: Courtesan and Spy* (New York, 1930); Richard Deacon, *A History of the British Secret Service* (New York, 1969), and *The Chinese Secret Service* (New York, 1976); Peer de Silva, *Sub Rosa: The CIA and Uses of Intelligence* (New York, 1978); James B. Donovan, *Strangers on a Bridge* (New York, 1976); Brian Freemangle, *KGB: Inside the World's Largest Intelligence Network* (New York, 1984); Reinhard Gehlen, *The Service* (New York, 1972); Anatoliy Golitsyn, *New Lies for Old* (New York, 1984); Anatoli Granovsky, *I Was An NKVD Agent* (New York, 1962); Louis Hagen, *The Secret War for Europe: A Dossier of Espionage* (New York, 1969); Baruch Hazan, *Soviet Impregnational Propaganda* (Ann Arbor, 1982); Allison Ind, *A Short History of Espionage* (New York, 1963); Nikolai Khikhlov, *In the Name of Conscience* (New York, 1959); David Lewis, *Sexpionage* (New York, 1976); Fitzroy Maclean, *Take Nine Spies* (New York, 1978); Pawel Monat, *Spy in the United States* (New York, 1961); Alan Moorhead, *The Traitors* (London, 1974); Bernard Newman, *The World of Espio-*

nage (New York, 1962); Liam O'Flaherty, *The Informer* (New York, 1961); Oleg Penkovskiy, *The Penkovskiy Papers* (New York, 1965); Walter Pforzheimer, editor, *Bibliography of Intelligence Literature* (Washington, Defense Intelligence College, 1985, eighth edition); Francis Gary Powers, *Overflight* (New York, 1970); Gordon W. Prange, *Target Tokyo: The Story of the Sorge Spy Ring* (New York, 1984); Harry Howe Ransom, *The Intelligence Establishment* (Cambridge, 1970); Anthony Read and David Fisher, *Colonel Z* (New York, 1985), and *Operation Lucy* (New York, 1981); Jeffrey T. Richelson, *The U.S. Intelligence Community* (Cambridge, 1985); Vladimir Sakharov, *High Treason* (New York, 1980); Ronald Seth, *Encyclopedia of Espionage* (London, 1972), and *Unmasked: The Story of Soviet Espionage* (New York, 1965); Bradley F. Smith, *The Shadow Warriors* (New York, 1983); John J. Stephan, *The Russian Fascists* (New York, 1978); Steven Stewart, *The Spymasters of Israel* (New York, 1980); Viktor Suvorov, *Inside Soviet Military Intelligence* (New York, 1984); Edward Van Der Rhoer, *The Shadow Network* (New York, 1973); Nigel West, *The Circus* (Briarcliff Manor, New York, 1983), *MI5* (London, 1981), *MI6* (New York, 1983), and *A Thread of Deceit* (New York, 1985); David Wise, *Spectrum* (New York, 1981); Thaddeus Wittlin, *Commissar: The Life and Death of Laventry Beria* (New York, 1972); Greville Wynne, *Contact on Gorky Street* (New York, 1968); and Allen Dulles, *The Craft of Intelligence* (New York, 1963). Government publications of value included Book One, "Foreign and Military Intelligence," of the Senate Select Committee to Study Governmental Activities with Respect to Intelligence Activities, 94th Congress, Second Session, Report 94-755, April 14, 1976 (The Church Committee, popularly); "Soviet Active Measures," House Permanent Select Committee on Intelligence, 97th Congress, Second Session, 1982; and "Communist Bloc Intelligence Activities in the United States," internal security subcommittee of the Senate Judiciary Committee, 94th Congress, First Session, 1975 (the testimony of Josef Frolik). The best overall volume on the history of intelligence remains Richard Wilmer Rowan, *The Story of Secret Service* (New York, 1937). And, finally, anyone who writes on the subject owes gratitude to Allen Dulles, *The Craft of Intelligence* (New York, 1963); Sherman Kent, *Strategic Intelligence for American World Policy* (Princeton, 1966, revised edition); and Lyman B. Kirkpatrick, Jr., *The U.S. Intelligence Community* (New York, 1973).

A Closing Note

The author intends to issue updated editions of *The Dictionary of Espionage* in coming years. Contributions would be gratefully received at the following address:

Sunshine Enterprises
2500 Que Street NW
Suite 320
Washington, DC 20007